Service Operations Dynamics

Henk Akkermans

Service Operations Dynamics

Managing in an Age of Digitization, Disruption and Discontent

Henk Akkermans
Tilburg University
Tilburg, The Netherlands

Foreword by Chris Voss
Warwick Business School
University of Warwick
Warwick, UK

ISBN 978-3-319-72016-6   ISBN 978-3-319-72017-3   (eBook)
https://doi.org/10.1007/978-3-319-72017-3

Library of Congress Control Number: 2018939156

Cover illustration: Pattern adapted from an Indian cotton print produced in the 19th century

Printed on acid-free paper

This Palgrave Pivot imprint is published by the registered company Springer International Publishing AG part of Springer Nature.
The registered company address is: Gewerbestrasse 11, 6330 Cham, Switzerland

He thought nothing less becoming in a well-trained leader than haste and rashness, and, accordingly, favorite sayings of his were: "Hasten slowly"; "Better a safe commander than a bold"; and "That which has been done well has been done quickly enough".

Suetonius, De vita Caesarum

The notion of festina lente, of combining speed with moderation, has a long history in mankind. The ancient Greeks had it as a proverb. The Roman emperor Augustus held it as his motto. In the Renaissance, this notion was symbolized by the intertwined symbols of the anchor and the dolphin, so combining stability and flexibility. In service operations management, it remains sound advice today.

FOREWORD

Technology and the need for rapid change are creating new challenges for the management of services. The classic approach to the management of service has been characterized by a focus on the service encounter, the service experience, the quality of the service, and the service employee. In recent years this has developed on three fronts. The first has been the broad area of e-services, including multichannel shopping and the Internet of Things. The second has been a focus on value creation and the related area of service-dominant logic. The third has been the recognition that any service should be considered as part of a broader ecosystem.

We have now moved into a new context. First is the growing digitization of services where increasingly services are IT enabled. Second, whilst the study of the management of service has focused on simple B2C (Business-to-Consumer) service, today it is important to think in terms of services, not just service, that are delivered by companies in every sector from government and publishing to aero engines. Next, there is a need to move on from just looking at the point of delivery; scholars may see value added through co-creation of service with customers, but the reality is that value comes from managing the whole service supply chain. This in turn means that management of services must have a wide discipline base that embracing marketing, operations, and systems.

Associated with digitization is the rapid pace of change; new services are increasingly launched in Beta to gain competitive advantage, and, at the industry level, companies have to change very rapidly—for example, manufacturing firms must embrace servitization, banks must become technology led, and textbook publishers must become digital educational service providers. All of this is creating enormous challenges: managing in a dynamic environment not just the front line, but the complex supply chains that are part of delivering today's services, and facing the challenges of IT-enabled services. The evidence from the field is that this is extremely difficult to achieve well.

The author of this book, Henk Akkermans, brings a unique combination of expertise and practice perspectives. First, a deep understanding of the dynamics of services combined with analytical expertise using system dynamics approaches. Second, a unique perspective based on a service supply chain view of services, and finally the learning from working with companies in a wide range of IT-enabled services. This book will provide both scholars and practitioners unique insights into how to manage services in today's dynamic and digitized context.

Professor of Operations Management   Chris Voss
Warwick Business School
Emeritus Professor of Management Science
and Operations, London Business School

Acknowledgments

Over the years, I learned so much from so many people, in business and academia. I will not try to mention all of them here. For the cases presented in this book and for the research on the basis of those, these are the people that were key, in alphabetical order: Greg Besio, Annelore Buijs, Peter Claerhoudt, Peggy Corstens, René de Vries, Paulo Gonçalves, Jacob Groote, Rene Heunen, Johan Hoek, Sjors Janssen, Daphne Jaspars-de Greeff, Marco van Katwijk, Anton Khoe, Eric Kuisch, Gerard van Laarhoven, Gerrit Loopstra, Rob Martens, Nat Mass, Frans van de Noort, Carol Ou, Roeland van Oers, Kishore Sengupta, Peter Trienekens, Ruud van Beeck, Kim van Oorschot, Luk van Wassenhove, Laurens Visser, Bart Vos, Chris Voss, Theo Wakkermans, Yan Wang, Finn Wynstra, Huub Zabel, and Quan Zhu.

Thank you for co-creating with me all those years.

Special mention deserves Willem van Oppen, *reflective practitioner* par excellence, with whom I have had the pleasure of working with for more than 15 years in the field of service operations. Many of the ideas on how to design and improve services in a collaborative process mentioned in this book are living examples of collaborative co-design between Willem and me.

Tilburg   Henk Akkermans
December 2017

CONTENTS

About the Author

Henk Akkermans For over 25 years, Henk Akkermans (1964) has been researching and providing consultation services to innovation-driven service companies in the industrial sectors of telecom, banking, insurance, utilities, and infrastructure. He was trained as an information analyst and industrial engineer. He looks at the processes that make service companies fail or succeed from a systemic perspective. This leads him to consider both the "soft" and the "hard" aspects of service operations. Most importantly, this makes him integrate both aspects.

He has published widely about his findings in leading academic journals. Presently he is a professor of supply chain management at Tilburg University. There he teaches the topics addressed in this book at the Master's and MBA level. He is also the Director of the World Class Maintenance Foundation in the Netherlands. Here he works with companies and institutions in the specific services area of maintenance and asset management to boost sustainable innovation.

He has written several books including *Supply Chain Dynamics* in 2015. He lives with his wife and children in Tilburg, the Netherlands.

LIST OF FIGURES

LIST OF TABLES

CHAPTER 1

Introduction

Abstract Services are the dominant mode of generating value in our economy but their dynamics remain poorly understood. How to manage operations is still derived from physical production processes. However, services are different. Moreover, IT is fundamentally changing services. In such IT-enabled service supply chains, volatility of demand and supply become much, much greater. And so, the need to understand how they really work and how to manage them is only becoming greater. This chapter introduces these fundamental challenges. Key in managing IT-enabled service operations is coordinating simultaneously between multiple stakeholders. Internally, this needs to take between Sales and Operations, but also between frontoffice and backoffice, and with Innovations. Externally, coordination needs to take place of course with customers, but also with key suppliers and even governmental regulators.

Services have been the dominant mode of generating value in our economy for several decades now. And still, services are poorly understood. The bulk of the theory and practice on how to manage operations is still derived from physical production processes. However, unlike physical products, services cannot be buffered or stored, and production and consumption are instantaneous, to mention two differences that have huge impact on how operations are best managed.

© The Author(s) 2018
H. Akkermans, *Service Operations Dynamics*,
https://doi.org/10.1007/978-3-319-72017-3_1

Moreover, things are changing. The biggest driver of change is IT. More and more services are becoming IT-enabled, they are digitized. They live in the Internet and are ordered from and/or delivered to mobile devices. This has made another aspect of services much more important: many services are delivered through a sequence of capacitated process steps, through a service supply chain. In such IT-enabled service supply chains, the volatility of demand and supply becomes much, much greater. IT-enabled service steps can easily grow by 100–1000%, but steps with human capacity as a bottleneck obviously cannot. And so, the need to understand how they really work and how to manage them is only becoming greater. We are talking about huge parts of the economy, affecting many millions of consumers: telecom providers, banks, insurance companies, energy utilities, the tax office, and other government institutions.

Unfortunately, at present there is only a limited amount of specialized academic literature available that offers guidance to practicing managers and to students of service operations. The goal of this textbook is to bundle and integrate these separate insights in a consistent and accessible manner for both operations students and operations executives.

1.1   Maintaining a Delicate Balance

This book tries to balance two opposing ideas. This balancing act is repeated a number of times. First, it combines insights from manufacturing operations with the unique nature of services. Our body of knowledge on manufacturing operations is vast and has accumulated over a century. There is much that service operations can learn from it, and this book indicates many links to these insights. On the other hand, services are intrinsically different from manufacturing. A very short summary of these fundamental differences is that service operations are *more difficult* to manage than manufacturing. This book also highlights these differences repeatedly.

Secondly, it balances theoretical insights with practical common sense. This book has its feet firmly on the ground and its head in the clouds. It has a sound empirical base of over a dozen cases of real-world companies facing problems with the dynamics of their service operations. At the same time, it also employs a wide array of theories and models, unified by a common system dynamics perspective. The theories and models provide the rigor that helps to understand the real world better. The cases assure the relevance of theories for the real world. The author has first-hand knowledge of all the cases in this book. He has worked as a consultant and/or action researcher in every one of them. He was also directly involved in all the formal models of the cases presented in this book. For the wonderful theories that place the case-specific phenomena in a broader perspective, various literatures were consulted. The author himself has contributed to several of these.

Thirdly, a recurrent theme in this book is that of *festina lente*. Service operations management requires balancing speed with thoughtfulness, two fundamentally opposed ideas it would seem. We will see that the managers in the cases we study most of the time err on the speed side; they try to go *too fast*. Or perhaps it is better said that they display *too little thoughtfulness*? This balancing act lies at the core of this book.

1.2   DIGITIZATION, DISRUPTION, AND DISCONTENT

This book is written because service operations especially are in dire need of better understanding and management. Services are faced with discontented customers, with disruption, and with digitization.

Discontented Customers

Services have had a bad name for at least two decades now: "services stink" (Brady 2000) or "bad service prevails" (Gerstner and Libai 2007). This is especially so in the business-to-consumer industries, which often serve hundred thousands to millions of consumers, and especially so in those services that are increasingly digitized, such as telecom, banking, insurance, utilities, and government services such as taxes.

This has been going on for at least two decades. Oliva and Sterman stated in 2001: "Erosion of service quality throughout the economy is a frequent concern in the popular press. The American Customer Satisfaction Index for services fell in 2000 to 69.4%, down 5 percentage points from 1994. We hypothesize that the characteristics of services—inseparability, intangibility, and labor intensity—interact with management practices to bias service providers toward reducing the level of service they deliver, often locking entire industries into a vicious cycle of eroding service standards."

Fifteen years later, the British consumer site thisismoney.co.uk writes this about the annual Wooden Spoon Award, a listing of firms that treat their customers badly: "So if you're brassed off with bungling banks, have been treated atrociously by telecoms giants or are fed up with being fobbed off by energy firms, now is your chance to get revenge" (www.thisismoney.co.uk 2015). Clearly, there is a problem.

Disruption and Digitization

One obvious explanation is that the waves of digitization and disruption have hit many service sectors hard since the 1990s. Senge (1990) already talks about problems with service quality in insurance. The oldest example from this book is from US telecom in 1995; the privatization waves of the 1990s hit many former government agencies hard. The financial crisis of 2008 has created turmoil for banking operations. The rapid succession of innovations in mobile telecom and Internet from recent years has made "disruption" an almost outdated buzzword.

All this is true, but this book will explain why services are hit much harder by all these new changes than manufacturing industries.

1.3   THE ROAD FORWARD

Paved with Good Intentions

Partly, disappointing service performance is the unintended side effect of good intentions. There are valid and understandable reasons why services haven't been doing better. Partly, this may be a conscious choice to diversify (Gerstner and Libai 2007). Mostly though, these are the unintended side effects of good intentions (law of unintended consequences or policy resistant issues) (Sterman 2000). Services have become so complex that very few managers of services have the skill set that is needed to do a good job.

A New and Unifying Perspective

This book aims to provide a new and unifying perspective to service operations that helps to provide the insights needed to do a better job. Throughout the chapters, it will become evident that this new perspective implies:

- Keeping a much broader range of stakeholders involved than the usual suspects, also involving secondary and tertiary processes.
- Managing from an integral perspective, and abolishing functional silos.
- Having a systemic understanding of the interdependencies between a host of factors, both soft and hard, with many dynamically complex elements such as feedback loops, time delays, and tipping points.
- Balancing a paradox of thoughtfulness and speed, what the Ancients called *festina lente*. In this book, *festina lente* is a recurrent theme in the analysis of why things went wrong. In most of the cases, management wanted things to go too fast, and did not deliberate enough about the drawbacks.

1.4   Structure of This Book

The chapters in this book are organized around the various stakeholders that the service operations function has to be aligned with.

Every chapter has a running case of a real-world setting where the interaction with this stakeholder in particular was very prominent. In our interconnected world there are always interactions with other stakeholders as well. This also applies to these running cases.

The cases come from the "repeat offenders" (www.thisismoney.co.uk 2015) of business-to-consumer services, including telecom (Chaps. 2, 3, 4 and 6), insurance (Chap. 5), utilities (Chap. 8), and government agencies (Chap. 7).

Every chapter focuses on managing a different type of stakeholder, as Fig. 1.1. illustrates:

- Chapter 2 focuses on the age-old coordination issues between Sales and Operations.
- Chapter 3 stresses the need for coordination between frontoffice and backoffice processes.
- Chapter 4 explains the risks of enraging the customer base.
- Chapter 5 shows the many interdependencies with the workforce.
- Chapter 6 looks at the interactions of service operations with the innovation ecosystem.
- Chapter 7 zooms in on the end customer service impact of key suppliers or co-makers.

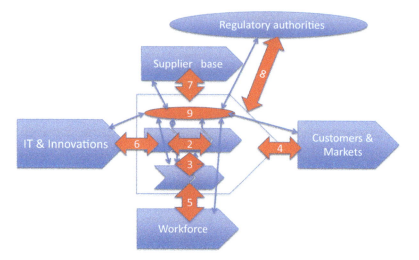

Fig. 1.1   The logic behind the structure of this book: managing stakeholders

- Chapter 8 illustrates the case of dealing with the regulatory authorities.
- Chapter 9 makes the case for managing all these stakeholders in an integrated and systemic manner.

The structure of every chapter is identical:

- First, a section on *what* happened and *what* went wrong.
- Then a section on *why* things happened, and why they went *wrong*. This is called the Root Causes section.
- Finally, a section on *how* things could be improved. These are labeled as Systemic Solutions.

For those interested in coordination issues with a specific stakeholder, or in a specific industry, feel free to jump directly to the specific chapter. Be aware though, that the other chapters may contain information that is relevant for your integral understanding.

REFERENCES

Brady, D. (2000, October 23). Why service stinks. *Business Week*.

Gerstner, E., & Libai, E. (2007). Why does poor service prevail? *Marketing Science, 25*(6), 601–603.

Oliva, R., & Sterman, J. D. (2001). Cutting corners and working overtime: Quality erosion in the service industry. *Management Science, 47*(7), 894–914.

Senge, P. (1990). *The fifth discipline: The art and practice of the learning organization*. New York: Doubleday.

Sterman, J. D. (2000). *Business dynamics: Systems thinking and modeling for a complex world*. New York: McGraw-Hill.

www.thisismoney.co.uk. (2015). Which firm drove you bonkers in 2015? http://www.thisismoney.co.uk/money/news/article-3351712/Which-firm-drove-bonkers-2015-Beware-bunglers-s-Wooden-Spoon-Awards-time-again.html#ixzz4mbrVNxkb

CHAPTER 2

Sales and Operations Interactions: *Never the Twain Shall Meet?*

Abstract This chapter looks at the classical misalignment between Sales and Operations. It sometimes looks like the two shall never meet. Digitization complicates matters further. Although services are becoming IT-enabled and fast-changing, they are still being delivered via compartmentalized service supply chains. Here, breakdowns in one stage amplify downstream, which makes it extremely difficult to maintain stability. These complications, and the challenges they pose to balancing sales with operations, are described with a case study of an American telecom company that was suffering from fluctuations in its service supply chain. The chapter provides a system dynamics analysis of the root causes of these fluctuations and also gives recommendations on how to maintain balance in this inherently unstable setting.

This chapter looks at a classical misalignment between two core stakeholders: sales and operations. Like East and West in the poem by Rudyard Kipling, it sometimes looks like the two shall never meet. This book is about services but this classical conflict has its roots in industrial organization. They go back to classical studies such as March and Simon's *Organizations* from 1958. To these authors, the root cause for interunit conflict is interdependence of units on the one hand and differences in objectives and perspectives at the other. One year later, still in the 1950s,

Table 2.1 Classical conflict areas between Sales and Operations

Problem area	Typical Sales comment	Typical Operations comment
Information flow		
Capacity planning and long-range sales forecasting	"Why don't we have enough capacity?"	"Why didn't we have accurate sales forecasts?"
Production scheduling	"Our leadtimes are too long"	"We need realistic customer commitments and stable sales forecasts"
Product flow		
Quality assurance	"Why can't we have reasonable quality at reasonable costs?"	"Why must we always offer options that are too hard to manufacture and that offer little customer utility?"
Breath of product line	"Our customers demand variety"	"The product line is too broad—all we get are short, uneconomical runs"
New product introduction	"New products are our life blood"	"Unnecessary design changes are very expensive"
Distribution	"Why don't we ever have the right products on stock?"	"We can't keep everything on stock"
Orientation		
Cost control	"Our costs are so high that we are not competitive"	"We can't provide fast delivery, high quality, broad variety at low costs"

Forrester published a classic system dynamics study called "Advertising, a problem in System Dynamics". We will find that this study has retained relevance in the decades that followed, including in the services context.

How do the problems between sales and operations manifest themselves? Through a number of conflict areas, which are aptly summarized in a table of typical quotes assembled by Konijnendijk (1992) in a synthesis of Shapiro (1977) and Powers et al. (1988) in Table 2.1. This same classical mismatch resonates in the first case of this book. This case is set in 1995, in the USA, and in a services context, not a manufacturing environment (Akkermans and Vos 2003).

2.1   A Service Supply Chain in Trouble

Services are typically delivered in a supply chain of subsequent stages. This structure makes them very vulnerable to disturbances. Our case dates back two decades, but this structural characteristic has not changed. The service supply chain under study was primarily responsible for providing new tele-com services to customers. It was also in trouble, for a number of reasons which are as relevant today as they were in 1995.

- Services are increasingly digitized and fast-changing.
- Services are delivered via compartmentalized supply chains.
- Breakdowns in one service supply chain stage amplify downstream.
- Service supply chains are extremely difficult to maintain stably.

Services Are Increasingly Digitized and Fast-Changing

Digitization changes services so fast that the people and the systems that have to deliver them cannot keep up with the rate of change. This is true today and was already true in 1995. Back then, by now legacy services such as ISDN were being introduced. Since then, technological develop-ments in telecom have been enormous, with huge increases in technology and functionality of the services. Examples include broadband Internet and fiber services, mobile devices, cloud solutions, and Internet of Things (IoT).

The telco we study was in many ways typical of its industry in the 1990s, a decade in which the telecom sector as a whole had been undergoing drastic changes as a result of deregulation and increased competition. These drastic changes in the telecom industry forced many companies to undergo profound organizational changes, involving substantial layoffs. Our case company had, in response to these turbulent times, taken two drastic steps. Externally, it had decided on an aggressive revenue growth strategy for new service products such as Caller ID, or Call Waiting, that is, these should ensure lock-in of customers, as the competition in the regular segments, such as long-distance calls and local calls, was becoming increasingly brutal. Sharp-pitched telesales campaigns played an important role in this marketing strategy, supported by strong advertising. As atten-tion spans of customers kept decreasing, these campaigns had to be intense, with a great deal of promotional activity happening in relatively short periods of time.

Services Are Delivered via Compartmentalized Supply Chains

Internally, an even more drastic step had been taken. The company had recently undergone a major Business Process Redesign (BPR) project involving major layoffs. As a result of this project, the organization was redefined into a number of key processes. One such process was the "establish customer service" process or ECS. The structure of the ECS process appears very similar to other service supply chains such as insurance (Senge 1990; Senge and Sterman 1992) or mortgage services (Anderson and Morrice 2000).

The four stages in our telecom case are all executed within the same organization. Still, clearly each of the four units within the telecom company had their own responsibility for controlling its own capacity. Thus, this case can be treated in a similar way as a supply chain where each stage is managed by a separate legal entity.

In organizations governed by functional "silos", the behavior of an internal service supply chain and that of an external supply chain are broadly the same. Also, in the manufacturing sector, similar results have been found in both settings. For instance, the famous "bullwhip effect" study by Lee et al. (1997) referred to the amplification of orders from one division of HP to the other. Earlier, both Van Aken (1978) and Hoekstra and Romme (1992) discussed the same phenomenon for a three-stage supply chain within the Philips organization (component manufacturer, assembler, and regional sales office). Both these studies reflect on the original study by Forrester (1961) of a four-stage manufacturing supply chain of General Electric.

Selling was the obvious first stage in this service chain. These activities, executed by sales agents, required both considerable technical skills and classical selling skills. The sales agent would also need to understand the specific characteristics of the product involved. In this stage, the company used a legacy mainframe system for order capturing, in which it was often cumbersome to note customer-specific details, especially for newer products. Therefore, hiring and training competent sales agents was a fairly lengthy process. The delays involved in the sales process itself were minimal; this process stage was designed to complete orders the same day.

Provisioning was the label for the internal (backoffice) activities that were started up after a sales order had been captured electronically. This involved manipulations in the internal systems of the company that regulated telecom traffic such as assigning new features to an existing number. This process was highly automated. However, if an error was detected that could not be solved by the computer, the order would literally "fall out" in paper format on the office floor. Human staff was then required to deal with it. Target delays in provisioning were minimal for flow-through orders, and 1–2 days for fallout orders.

Installing is the process stage in which actual visits to customer sites were made to physically install telecom equipment, such as an additional line. Not all new telecom services required actual field visits. Services such as call waiting or voice mail could move from the provisioning stage straight to billing. About one-third of new services that needed field visits required a substantial labor force of skilled service technicians. Hiring and proper training of technicians was a lengthy process. The installing process was designed in such a way that, under normal conditions, an installation visit would take 3 days for planning and executing.

Billing was an activity that was only partially covered by this particular service supply chain. Again, as in provisioning, this was a heavily automated process in which most of the staff were there to correct errors. Obviously, the vast majority of bills that any telecom company sends out every month are bills for repeated services. The initial billing process stage covered by the ECS process entailed preparing and sending out the first bill for the new service. Sending out these initial bills took place at the end of the month; so the billing delay was designed to be half a month on average.

Breakdowns in One Service Supply Chain Stage Amplify Downstream

In supply chains, the bullwhip effect is always active (Lee et al. 1997). This is a dynamic phenomenon where changes in one stage of the supply chain become greater, *amplified* in the next stage. A similar effect is active in service supply chains: the service bullwhip effect (Akkermans and Voss 2013). In the spring of 1995, it was clear that the ECS process was experiencing such effects. It had experienced severe order backlog and workload fluctuations in the past year. Three examples of such fluctuations were the following:

1. During a sales campaign for several "hot" and new complex products, a huge amount of errors occurred in entering sales orders. This was partly caused by the work pressure, the lack of training of the sales staff,

and the outdated functionality of the order processing system. This system needed complex and technical codes to activate specific customer features and, in general, was fairly inflexible and user-unfriendly. Under pressure to close the deal, sales agents would put everything they could not immediately place in their input screen in the input field for "comments", where it would not be recognized by the automated systems in provisioning. Consequently, the increase in overall order volume was around 10% of normal volume but the increase in workload was several times that percentage. So, clearly, amplification occurred, because the response of the output signal was far greater than the change in the input signal.

2. During a computer malfunctioning in one of the regional provisioning centers, an event that was internally called a "meltdown" occurred. This implied that in a few days' time, a huge stock of backlog accumulated because large numbers of sales orders were rejected. Despite massive overtime and additional capacity from other centers, it took over half a year to get workloads more or less back to normal. So, again, the change in the output signal (several months of higher workload in the provisioning center) was far greater than the original change in the input signal (some days of computer malfunctioning).

3. During extreme weather conditions in a winter storm, a host of errors occurred in "plain old telephony services" (POTS) operations. Because of one period of bad weather, call centers became practically inaccessible, with queue times of up to an hour. It took the company weeks to make the necessary emergency fixes and then a much longer time to return to normal working hours and workloads again. Again, a change in the input signal of a day resulted in an amplification in the output signal (workload in installation) of a considerably greater magnitude.

Such amplification phenomena are not specific to one business or company in one region in one particular time period. Figure 2.1 shows clear amplification effects in a service supply chain for glass fiber network services from a European telco in the 2007–2009 period. It also shows the potentially long delays between a peak in one stage and a peak in the next stage. Such delays make it even harder to understand what is really happening. In this case, the install rates went up over half a year after the peak of contracting out work to outside contractors. This is because it took the contractors half a year to process this peak in work. By the time the work

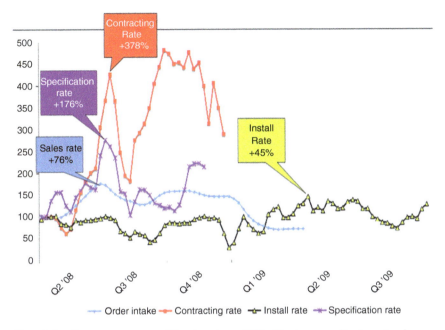

Fig. 2.1 Downstream amplification in a B2B (Business-to-Business) telecom service supply chain

backlog came back to the telco's field install technicians, this group had already been downsized. After all, for half a year this staff did not have much work to do.

Service Supply Chains Are Inherently Unstable

It is extremely difficult to maintain stability in service supply chains when they are put under pressure. For the ECS process, a simulation analysis revealed what the effects were of a sales campaign on workload in each of the processes. Table 2.2 shows the maximum workload as a result of a sudden increase of 10% in sales activity. Here it becomes clear that what seems like a modest increase upstream can become a huge increase in work downstream.

When put under pressure, it is almost impossible to keep capacities and processing rates at every stage in the supply chains aligned. Now it is time to look at why this is.

Table 2.2 Amplification ratios per stage as a result of a major sales campaign (from Akkermans and Vos 2003)

Supply chain stage	Workload steady state	Max workload after 10% sales increase	% increase in workload
Sales	0.25	0.29	14
Provisioning	0.83	2.95	254
Install	1.32	3.20	142
Billing	0.95	2.65	175

2.2   ROOT CAUSES: SERVICES, SILOS, AND SYSTEMS

The root causes for the problems that service supply chains face are fundamental and wide-ranging. In the present chapter we will address four: [In the coming chapters we will look at others]

- Services have more complex characteristics than manufacturing.
- Services are plagued by functional silos and short-term biases.
- Service supply chains exhibit complex behavior.
- Service IT systems are inadequate to deal with the managerial tasks effectively.

Services Are Different

Services operations are fundamentally different from manufacturing operations. These characteristics make them inherently more vulnerable to disturbances. Pure services are intangible, labor-intensive, and heterogeneous. They cannot be stored and transported because production and consumption occur simultaneously, they have a high level of customer influence, and they have a quality dimension that is often difficult to judge (Nie and Kellogg 1999; Foster et al. 2000; Slack et al. 2001).

As a result, effective operations management of services is more difficult than for manufacturing operations:

- One cannot buffer against fluctuations with stock.
- One can only buffer with capacity, because service is instantaneous.
- The customer co-produces with most steps of the service delivery process, so quality glitches cannot be hidden.

- Service capacity planning is much more difficult than MRP as service capacity demands cannot be calculated from order quantities.

Services Cannot Be Buffered

In manufacturing, stocks of finished goods are often used to buffer against unpredictable customer demand. This is impossible with most services. Services are intangible and so cannot be stored (Chase 1996). There is no way for stakeholders in such chains to use finished goods inventories as a buffer against demand fluctuations (see Anderson and Morrice 2000; Sampson 2000; Akkermans and Vos 2003). Rather, backlogs of orders are created that can be managed through service capacity adjustments. Each process stage can only control its backlog by managing its capacity, being the number of people it employs. In adjusting capacity levels, it takes time to interview, hire, and train new employees who are capable of providing high-quality services to customers.

This is visualized in a more formal manner in the stocks-and-flows diagram (Sterman 2000) in Fig. 2.2. When there are more customer orders coming in than can be filled, the Order Backlog grows. How many orders can be filled depends on the available capacity. Available capacity is the product of the staff available and their productivity. How much staff is needed depends on the workload that is currently experienced. How fast staff adjusts depends on the delays associated with it. These include hiring but also training. The missing variable in this model is inventory, since services are intangible and cannot be stored.

Services Are Co-Produced by Customers and Suppliers

Services are characterized by customer contact in service processes (Chase 1978) and by co-creation of value between supplier and customer (Vargo and Lusch 2004). This may result in two-way flows between customers and suppliers (Sampson 2000).

Direct interaction with customers is common for service operations. An example is a financial services company providing tailor-made pension arrangements for its customers. Such service processes require direct and intense customer contacts. Sampson (2000) refers to this characteristic as the customer-supplier duality: all services have customers as primary suppliers of inputs.

This makes service supply chains much more exposed to customer scrutiny during their "production" than manufacturing supply chains. If a smartphone experienced some problems during its production, its buyer

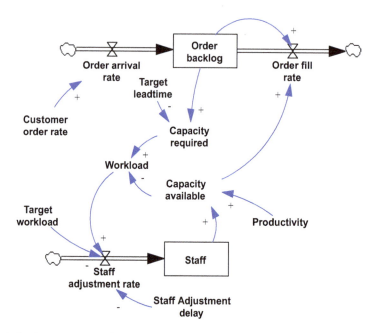

Fig. 2.2 Interactions of order backlog, staff, capacity, and workload. (Adapted from Akkermans and Vos 2003)

will never know. If there are problems during the ordering of a mobile telecom subscription, the customer will probably notice this. So, every step of the service delivery process has to be right to delight the customer.

Of course, not all stages in the service delivery process have direct customer involvement. There will still be backoffice processes of service companies that function very much like a factory, without customers observing every step of the way (Chase 1996).

Service Supply Chains Are Very Difficult to Plan

In manufacturing supply chains, integral capacity coordination has long been possible because of the connecting aspect of the physical goods flow. If there is an order volume for *X* products arriving in week *T*, then one can calculate with the planning Bill of Material what the capacity and material requirements are for every step of the supply chain in the weeks *T*+*n* (Orlicky 1975). However, for service supply chains this is simply not feasible.

One example is the capacity planning for the field install technicians in the current telecom case. Broadly speaking, one can still assume that if X customer orders have arrived in week T, that there needs to be capacity to install X customer orders in week $T+n$. Here n stands for the number of weeks it takes to process sales orders and conduct the required provisioning work, the two supply chain stages that precede Field Install. However, how much work those orders actually are will crucially depend on the quality of the execution of these two prior stages. In this case, many sales orders were entered incorrectly in the order handling system. Many orders fell out of the Provisioning stage with errors associated with it. Such rework orders also led to rework in field install, and so to much lower productivity. It may also change the value of n. And field install is still a relatively straightforward step. How about estimating the required capacity at the Complaints department, or Customer Care in general? What is the direct link there between sales orders in week T and capacity demands in week $T+n$?

Functional Silos and Short-Term Thinking

Service operations have been demarcated into separate silos and these silos are mostly managed in isolation, which is wrong. Moreover, they are mostly managed with a short-term orientation, which is also wrong. The problem of complicated or not impossible planning tasks was less of an issue in the old, regulated days. Then, the rate of innovation was low, there were no steep targets on sales, and there were many buffers of excess staff. So, order volumes were less volatile and so easier to plan. And when there was volatility, there was excess capacity as a buffer.

This all changed in the 1990s in US telecom, and has changed throughout the Western world in all service sectors since then. The classical dichotomy between sales and operations was reinforced because both functions were more strictly evaluated against their own performance. Sales had to sell more and Operations had to trim its buffer capacities. They were evaluated against their own functional targets: sales against new revenue and operations against costs. No function was evaluated against integral performance, against first-time-right orders, for instance.

Short-term thinking made things worse. The drive to meet quarterly targets or certainly annual targets motivated sales campaigns in autumn when Operations capacity was already tight due to weather conditions and the upcoming Christmas season. The drive to cut costs quickly by firing employees made the operations function more vulnerable to future swings in demand.

Shapiro, Rangan, and Sviokla summarized this miserable state of affairs back in 1992: "At company after company, we traced the progress of individual orders (...). What we witnessed was frustration, missed opportunities, dissatisfied customers, and underperforming companies" (Shapiro et al. 1992, p. 117). These functional goals were developed to make companies more efficient. However, they achieve the opposite. "We saw companies lose sales, waste labor, and fumble investments because of poor management cycles. Typically, companies throw money at their problems, building excess capacities, adding inventory, or increasing the body count, all of which are expensive and none of which solve the real problem" (Shapiro et al. 1992, p. 122). A quarter of a century later, this situation is not fundamentally different in many service settings.

Service Supply Chains Exhibit Complex Behavior

Service supply chains are complex dynamic systems that behave in non-intuitive ways. This is the third reason why the telco that we study in this chapter, and so many service companies after it, failed to manage service operations well. Service operations are a special case of dynamic systems, entities with relations between them that change over time. We are accustomed to studying physical dynamic systems, such as airplanes or bicycles. We find it logical that scientists and engineers develop mathematical models of those systems to study them. With those models they can run experiments that would be risky, expensive, or simply impossible and learn from those experiments. We find such an attitude to controlling technical dynamic systems normal. Since the late 1950s, the field of *system dynamics* studies social systems from the same perspective (Forrester 1959, 1961; Sterman 2000). This book applies this same system dynamics perspective to the management of service operations.

From a system dynamics perspective, it is evident that service supply chains exhibit certain characteristics that make it complex to manage them well. These include:

Feedback Loops

There are two kinds of feedback loops. There is negative and positive feedback. Positive does not mean "good"; it means that there is a positive relation between two variables. So, if workload is high, burnout will grow.

Fig. 2.3 An example of a positive/reinforcing feedback loop

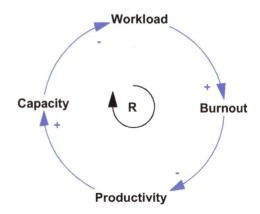

That is a "positive relation". If more burnout will lead to lower productivity, that is a negative relationship. If lower productivity then goes on to lead to lower capacity (positive relation) and from there on to higher workload (negative), then we have a positive or reinforcing feedback loop, because higher workload will lead to even more burnout, and so on. We usually denote this feedback loop with a special sign of a curved arrow and an "R" in the middle. This is visualized in Fig. 2.3.

Negative feedback loops are of the regulating kind. They try to balance situations. For instance, higher workload leads to more hires, which leads to more capacity which leads to lower workloads which leads to fewer hires needed. This is illustrated in Fig. 2.4. A balancing loop is denoted by a curved arrow with a "B" for balancing in its middle. Please note that there is a "negative" relation between capacity and workload, but this is not a "bad" thing, just a negative correlation between these two variables.

Combinations of negative and positive feedback loops regulate all social systems, as also service operations systems. Will workload and burnout continue to grow or will the balancing feedback loop kick in timely? One cannot tell; that will depend on other aspects of dynamic systems, such as the ones discussed below.

Time Delays
Another key aspect of dynamic systems is that it takes time for things to change. It takes time for burnout to build up. And time for burnout to affect productivity and thereby capacity. It also takes time to find, recruit,

Fig. 2.4 An example of a negative/balancing feedback loop

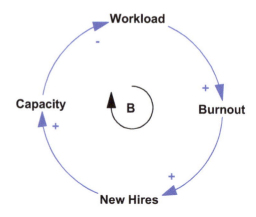

and train new hires. What the net result will be of a period of high workloads depends on which of these two loops will be "fastest" and will have the shortest time delays associated with it. Similarly, it will take time for latent upstream errors to become visible in downstream operations. It will take time for customers to become enraged with bad performance. Delays are everywhere in service operations, and understanding them is crucial for performance.

Nonlinearity
Another aspect that complicates management of dynamic systems is that they do *not* behave *linearly*, whereas most of our spreadsheet analyses assume linearity. For example, there is no linear relation between an extra car on the road and the extent of the delay due to heavy traffic. One can add many cars on an empty road without any effect at all on traffic delays. Only once a critical load of cars on the road is reached does one observe a fast-growing increase in the size of the traffic jam. That growth is nonlinear. Similarly, a modest increase in workload will have no effect on burnout. Only high workloads sustained over longer time periods will have such effects. Again, the effects are nonlinear.

Service IT Systems Are Inadequate

As the services themselves become more digitized, the IT systems that have to manage them increasingly lag behind in sophistication. This applies to both the transactional systems and the management systems. By *transac-*

tional we mean the IT systems that support the actual executions of the services themselves. These include the logging of a new sales order, or the provisioning system that links a phone number to a physical location or a mobile device, or the workflow system that tells a service technician what job to perform next. And certainly also the billing system which sends out the invoice to charge for the service rendered. By *managerial* we mean the IT systems that help to manage and control the service operations.

What we do *not* mean is the IT inherent to the service itself. More and more, services become digitized. Watching TV over the Internet is a fully digitized service. So is browsing, or streaming of music. In services, progress in digitization has been tremendous.

In services, the quality of both transactional and managerial IT systems still leaves much to be desired. Back in 1995, this was even more true than today. But even today the situation is far from perfect. Back in 1995, it was not possible for the telco to input order data for certain new kinds of services correctly into the mainframe-based sales order IT system. However, as we will see in subsequent chapters, most transactional systems in services are still a patchwork of individual applications, with unstable interfaces between them and lousy data consistency. This makes errors in the order processing processes inevitable. Designing error-free workflows appears to be very difficult indeed.

This is certainly one explanation why managerial IT systems for service operations still lag behind. It is, however, not the only one. They may explain the first of the following reasons to some extent, but not the others:

- No transparency of performance (backlogs, capacities, workloads) across the service supply chain.
- Difficult to translate capacity requirements from one stage to another.
- No measurement of error rates, and rework and associated time delays often not measured.
- Insufficient tracking of development over time.

To illustrate the last two points, here is an example from another telco a decade later. Here too, there were issues in the service delivery process. One area to look for root causes was the Provisioning stage in the service supply chain. Data on what orders fell out and so needed to be reworked could not be found in the standard performance dashboards available to management. A specific data query could come up with the rates of order fallout and order rework shown in Fig. 2.5.

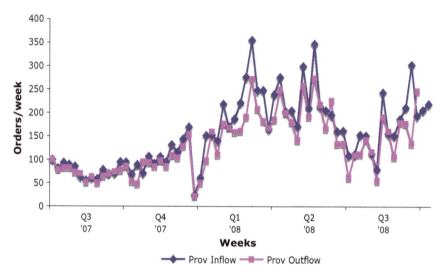

Fig. 2.5   Provisioning rework inflow and outflow

This graph was unusual for managerial reports because of its long time horizon. Normally, only the last few weeks or days would be reported, making it impossible to see longer trends. The longer trend here seems to be of a rise in rework from Q4 2007 onwards, peaking in Q1–Q2 of 2008, and then becoming less towards Q3. That in itself was news enough for management, but the response was still "we knew that".

However, there is also a picture of the *accumulated* backlog of provisioning rework that can be drawn when the net difference between inflow and outflow is added up over time. This is shown in Fig. 2.6. That graph shows a much more disturbing picture of a steady accumulation of problems that does not diminish. These problems were not being seen and so were not being addressed and led to major customer issues in 2008 (Akkermans and Voss 2013).

2.3   Systemic Solutions

The solutions to these problems are in many cases mirror images of the problems observed in this case. In order to align Sales and Operations well in dynamic service supply chains, the following four approaches are all required:

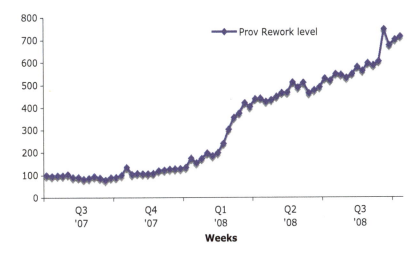

Fig. 2.6 Accumulated backlog of provisioning rework

- A systemic perspective
- A cross-functional approach
- A quality-first orientation
- A *festina lente* approach to growth

A Systemic Perspective

A systemic perspective is precisely what the manager of the ECS process in the case in this chapter wanted to achieve. In her words, she wanted "to see how the moving parts work together". This is why she commissioned the system dynamics modeling study that the author was involved in (Akkermans and Vos 2003). This lack of systemic insights is regrettably the normal situation. In subsequent chapters we will see that it still is so two decades after this case. However, already in 1992, Shapiro et al. noted: "Most companies never view the Order Management Cycle as a whole system. People in sales think that someone in production scheduling understands the entire system; people in production scheduling think customer service reps do. No one really does, and everyone can only give a partial description" (Shapiro et al. 1992, p. 117).

Senge (1990) called this the need to see the "the whole elephant" in complex dynamic settings. Why is it that nobody has a thorough view of the entire size of the issues? Partly because it is simply too much, but also because it is nobody's job to do so. To top management, the details of the service supply chain are invisible. Senior executives simply don't understand all the intricacies of the operational processes. And people with the most crucial information, such as customer service reps, are at the bottom of the organization and can't communicate with the top (Shapiro et al. 1992).

Simply sending data up the chain of command doesn't work either. As Ackoff already noted in 1967: one cannot specify what information managers need to make the right decisions until "an explanatory model of the decision process and the system involved has been constructed and tested" (Ackoff 1967, p. B-150).

A Cross-Functional Approach

The various functions need to work together to make the service supply chain as a whole perform optimally, and not to suboptimize their own function. To encourage such alignment, managers have a number of tools at their disposal; Shapiro et al. (1992) mention three of those tools:

- *The company compensation system.* Managers can use this to introduce joint reward plans that encourage employees to take a system-wide view of company performance.
- *Performance measurements for departments.* Managers can include numbers that reflect performance across boundaries or throughout the system.
- *Interdepartmental projects.* "Projects that cross department boundaries can create an integrated atmosphere. Significantly, interdepartmental projects, usually underfunded for years, often deliver the greatest returns to the company in terms of real improvements and financial results" (Shapiro et al. 1992, p. 121).

Marjchrzak and Wang (1996) also mention incentive systems, but they add other measures as well:

- *Organizational routines.* "Reconfiguring the work space, or designing jobs and procedures (…) to encourage collaboration and collective responsibility" (Marjchrzak and Wang 1996, p. 95).

- *Functional mindset of managers.* Many managers do away with functions but fail to change their own positions. They continue to act like functional chiefs even when these functions no longer formally exist.
- *Organizational culture.* Many managers "fail to see that collective responsibility is an attitude, a value, a concern. It means taking an interest in one's colleagues and in improving the outcome of mutual (as opposed to individual) efforts. People who feel collectively responsible are willing to work especially hard to avoid letting the team down" (Marjchrzak and Wang 1996, p. 95).

A Quality-First Orientation

It seems such a subtle difference, but it is fundamental: *Focus on cost, quality goes down; focus on quality, costs go down* (Akkermans and van Oppen 2006). In an effort to cut costs, buffer capacity in the form of experienced technical staff had been removed from the company. The result was that quality suffered and that, as a result of all the rework, costs still went up. What was needed was a quality-first orientation. This of course resonates with the quality management principles from Toyota (Ohno 1988), the lean movement (Womack et al. 1990), and perhaps even lean six sigma (George 2003). These all focus on the reduction of waste as a way of reducing costs, and on waste as basically the result of shortcomings in quality.

Therefore, the best policy for the ECS process would have been to focus on consistently high quality. In the policy analyses that were run with the simulation model that was developed for this process this was the one policy that proved to be robust and successful. Consistently high-quality means to have high incoming quality from sales orders and to have operational work procedures immune to quality drops as a result of high workloads (Akkermans and Vos 2003). We will look into this more in detail in the next chapter.

A Festina Lente *Approach to Growth*

It is understandable that top management and sales in particular were in a hurry to capture the opportunities in a new and fast-growing market. But, as the Greeks and Romans already knew, there is merit in haste with moderation. Having a major advertising campaign in the months before Christmas sounds like a great idea to meet end-of-year revenue targets.

However, when this leads to extra work in the winter, when staff is on holiday and there is much unplanned maintenance work because of weather conditions, this may not be such a smart idea after all.

The step back from the process that the responsible manager ordered, to see how all the moving parts fit together, was a lot smarter. This led to an insight into where all the real "leverage points" in the system were. And we will see again and again in this book that this was good advice.

2.4   CONCLUSION

Service operations are best seen as service supply chains. However, there are both similarities and differences between service supply chains and manufacturing supply chains. Similarities are that in both settings alignment of sales and operations is crucial. Another similarity is that this is often difficult because of the functional mindset that governs many organizations, and because of the dynamic complexity of the supply chain.

A difference is that service supply chains are inherently more complex and unstable than manufacturing supply chains. They can exhibit wilder volatilities than manufacturing supply chains. Several of the mitigating policies, such as buffering against uncertainties through inventories, are not possible with services.

What is needed is an integral approach, one that cuts across functions and organizational boundaries, and that manages the entire service supply chain as a system. A focus on quality before costs, and a focus on moderation before haste are good advice for all supply chains, but certainly for those *wild* service supply chains that simultaneously face disruption, digitization, and discontented customers.

REFERENCES

Ackoff, R. L. (1967). Management misinformation systems. *Management Science, 14*(4), 147–156.

Akkermans, H. A, & van Oppen, W. (2006). *Offensive KPIs: Improving buyer-supplier collaboration in inter-organizational service supply networks.* Proceedings International System Dynamics Conference, Radboud University, The Netherlands. Accessible at www.systemdynamics.org

Akkermans, H. A., & Vos, C. J. G. M. (2003). Amplification in service supply chains: An exploratory case study from the telecom industry. *Production and Operations Management, 12*(2), 204–223.

Akkermans, H. A., & Voss, C. (2013). The service bullwhip effect. *International Journal of Production and Operations Management, 33*(6), 765–788.

Anderson, E. G., & Morrice, D. J. (2000). A simulation game for teaching service-oriented supply chain management: Does information sharing help managers with service capacity decisions? *Production and Operations Management, 9*(1), 40–55.

Chase, R. B. (1978). Where does the customer fit in a service operation? *Harvard Business Review, 56*(6), 137–142.

Chase, R. B. (1996). The mall is my factory: Lessons from a service junkie. *Production and Operations Management, 5*(4), 298–308.

Forrester, J. W. (1959). Advertising-A problem in industrial dynamics. *Harvard Business Review, 37*(2), 100–110.

Forrester, J. W. (1961). *Industrial dynamics.* Cambridge, MA: MIT Press.

Foster, S. T., Sampson, S. E., & Dunn, S. C. (2000). The impact of customer contact on environmental initiatives for service firms. *International Journal of Operations and Production Management, 20*(2), 187–203.

George, M. L. (2003). *Lean six sigma for service.* New York: McGraw-Hill.

Hoekstra, S., & Romme, J. (Eds.). (1992). *Integral logistic structures, developing customer-oriented goods flow.* Maidenhead: McGraw Hill.

Konijnendijk, P. A. (1992). *Coordination of production and sales.* PhD thesis, TU Eindhoven.

Lee, H. L., Padmanabhan, V., & Whang, S. (1997). Information distortion in a supply chain: The bullwhip effect. *Management Science, 43*(4), 546–558.

March, J., & Simon, H. (1958). *Organizations.* New York: Wiley.

Marjchrzak, A., & Wang, Q. (1996). Breaking the functional mind-set in process organizations. *Harvard Business Review, 74*(5), 93–99.

Nie, W. and D. Kellogg, D. (1999) How professors of operations management view service operations? Production and Operations Management 8(3), 339–355.

Ohno, T. (1988). *Toyota production system: Beyond large-scale production.* Cambridge, MA: Productivity Press.

Orlicky, J. (1975). *Material requirements planning.* New York: McGraw-Hill.

Powers, T. L., Sterling, J. U., & Wolter, J. F. (1988). Marketing and manufacturing conflict: Sources and resolution. *Production and Inventory Management Journal, 1*(1), 56–60.

Sampson, S. E. (2000). Customer-supplier duality and bi-directional supply chains in service organizations. *International Journal of Service Industry Management, 11*(4), 348–364.

Senge, P. (1990). *The fifth discipline: The art and practice of the learning organization.* New York: Doubleday.

Senge, P., & Sterman, J. (1992). Systems thinking and organizational learning: Acting locally and thinking globally in the organization of the future. *European Journal of Operational Research, 59*(1), 137–150.

Shapiro, B. P. (1977, September-October). Can marketing and manufacturing coexist? *Harvard Business Review, 55,* 104–114.

Shapiro, B. P., Rangan, V. K., & Sviokla, J. J. (1992, July–August). Staple yourself to an order. *Harvard Business Review, 70,* 113–122.

Slack, N., Chambers, S., & Johnston, R. (2001). *Operations management* (3rd ed.). Harlow: Pearson Education Limited.

Sterman, J. D. (2000). *Business dynamics: Systems thinking and modeling for a complex world.* New York: McGraw-Hill.

Van Aken, J. E. (1978). *On the control of complex industrial organizations.* Leiden: Martinus Nijhoff Social Sciences Division.

Vargo, S. L., & Lusch, R. F. (2004). Evolving towards a new dominant logic for marketing. *Journal of Marketing, 68,* 1–17.

Womack, J. P., Jones, D. T., & Roos, D. (1990). *The machine that change the world.* New York: Harper Collins.

CHAPTER 3

Frontoffice-Backoffice Interactions: *Service Quality Cascades*

Abstract In service supply chains, disturbances amplify from one stage to another. In the current chapter we find that on top of this a further complication occurs. When workloads in the frontoffice become stressed, quality in backoffice processes suffers even more. Frontoffice staff will make more errors under stress. Those extra errors lead to more backoffice rework, which further increases workloads. This then gets amplified in other stages, as quality issues and workloads cascade down the service supply chain. Workloads become especially stressed during the volume ramp-up phase for new services. We therefore look at some examples of unsuccessful new service introductions.

In service supply chains, disturbances amplify from one stage to another. In the current chapter we find that on top of this a further complication occurs. When workloads in the frontoffice become stressed, quality in backoffice processes suffers even more. Frontoffice staff will make more errors under stress. Those extra errors lead to more backoffice rework, which further increases the workload. This is then also amplified to other stages, as quality issues and workloads cascade down the service supply chain. Workloads become especially stressed during the volume ramp-up phase for new services. We therefore look at some examples of unsuccessful new service introductions.

© The Author(s) 2018
H. Akkermans, *Service Operations Dynamics*,
https://doi.org/10.1007/978-3-319-72017-3_3

3.1   MORE CANCELLATIONS THAN ORDERS

Here is a case of a company confident it had made all the right moves and, nevertheless, saw its ramp-up end as a disaster. This case is set around 2010 in Europe in a mid-sized telecom company. The service in question is a combination of broadband Internet and Voice over Internet Protocol (VoIP) telephony for small to medium-sized enterprises. Its service supply chain structure is comparable to the case setting in the preceding chapter. It too had an upstream and a downstream stage, preceded by sales activities.

The upstream stage was mostly IT enabled. This means that only for its rework did it depend on human capacity. The downstream stage invariably involved human capacity for field installation activities. Figure 3.1 shows the two main stages "Order Preparation" and "Order processing". Both stages have a backlog, which can be significant when the outflow stays significantly below the inflow for a number of weeks. In both stages, cancellations can occur, triggered either by the customer or by the service provider.

The company made three consecutive attempts to ramp up this service. We will examine longitudinal data for these attempts. For each ramp-up we show data for order intake, order backlog, cancellation rates, fulfillment rates, and the installed base, (absolute numbers are disguised for reasons of confidentiality).

The Nursery Room Concept

The company had learned a lesson from dramatic new service introductions in the past. It would not ramp up this new service before it was

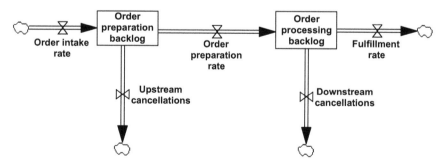

Fig. 3.1 Stylized process flow for the service supply chain under study

absolutely sure that the service supply chain was working fine. To test this, it set up what was called a "nursery room". Here, key staff from sales, provisioning, IT, customer care, field install, billing, and so on, were co-located on the same office floor. Thus communication lines regarding individual orders were very short. From this location they made sure that orders from customers proceeded apparently seamlessly through the order handling system. Even more importantly, they assured the actual delivery of the new service to the customer. Problems they encountered were fed back to the IT development team. Concurrently, the company was developing a bespoke order processing workflow system. IT innovation was a major element in this stage, since the various software systems involved were—obviously—not yet mature, and this first ramp-up certainly also served as a means of testing how all these newly developed systems would perform together in practice.

This is where the first ramp-up was conducted. The results are shown in Fig. 3.2. Order intake started quietly. Order backlog remained fairly stable, until it could be brought down significantly through successful order fulfillment in time. As a result, it was felt safe to ramp up more rapidly. Order intake was doubled and then doubled again in this quarter. How many new contracts were sold could be regulated through the use of outbound sales.

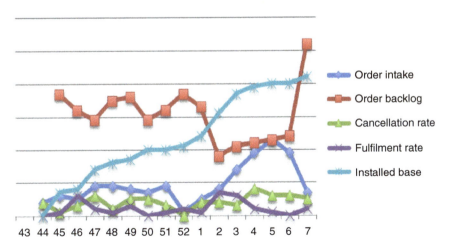

Fig. 3.2 First ramp-up from the "nursery room"

However, the rise in new orders soon led to problems. Various quality issues arose and hardly any orders were completed. Instead, the only outflow of backlog occurred through cancellations. Those cancellations were from dissatisfied customers and from the company itself. The company cancelled orders when it became obvious that there were too many technical impediments to provide the service that had been sold earlier. So, order intake was strongly reduced and a few weeks later effectively brought to a halt.

In the months that followed, workflows and IT support for those was redesigned. The few dozen orders that had been processed so far were reprocessed to test the new workflow.

Ramp-Up in Sales, Not in Deliveries

Some 30 weeks after the start of the nursery room initiative, a workshop called "Risk Management Business VoIP Chain" was held. Here, the author played the role of an external expert. The examples from disastrous earlier ramp-ups within the company were once more presented. Also, the lessons learned from these were discussed. The conclusion of this workshop was, however, that all the risks voiced were under control.

So just 2 months later, the actual ramp-up was started. The company was ready for a real attempt to process the order volume needed to start capturing the market with this innovative and attractive new service.

The order intake exploded for the next 2–3 months. During this brief period, sales managed to swamp the service operations. Order backlog became filled with more orders than downstream operations could handle in a year. During this tenfold rise in contracted new sales, there was virtually no increase in the rate of service activations. This fact completely escaped the attention of management, in particular of sales management. Meanwhile, leadtimes soared and customer dissatisfaction went through the roof. Management was in crisis. What had gone wrong?

Fragmented Downstream Orders

A single sales order upstream fragmented into a myriad of specific jobs in downstream operations. This was not a service for a consumer household, but for a small to medium business. Business requirements are more complex than consumer requirements. As a result, many specific jobs had to be conducted, all at different times and often by different capacity groups. Cables had to be laid, which meant permits needed to be obtained, contractors to dig sledges had to be found, and so on. Within all these individual orders, it was very hard to achieve transparency in overall progress. So Fig. 3.1 provides a stylized depiction. In reality, these two steps entailed a highly complex set of up to a 100 separate activities, enabled by over 50 independent IT systems.

This means that it was very difficult to monitor progress on these orders. They simply "disappeared" from the frontoffice into lots and lots of backoffice processes. This is also visible in Fig. 3.3, which shows that the fulfillment backlog and backoffice work remained high for a long time. In contrast, the upstream order backlog, which was mostly frontoffice work, was fairly quickly depleted.

Long Leadtimes

As a result of far more inflow than outflow of orders, leadtimes became excessively long, which led to high customer dissatisfaction.

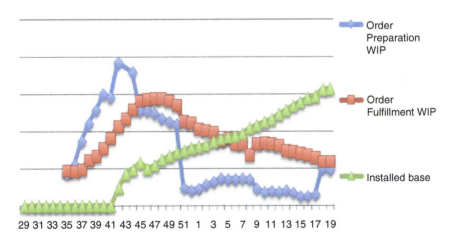

Fig. 3.3 Frontoffice versus backoffice order backlogs and installed base during large-scale ramp-up

Unfortunately the fulfillment rates stayed far below the intake rates and the backlog only grew. Order backlog only stopped growing not so much through an increase in the number of orders activated, but more through an increase in the number of cancellations and, most significantly, through a drop in the size of the new contracting rate. Order backlog remained very high and leadtimes in this period were between 11 and 15 weeks.

Massive Cancellations

Many customers decided to cancel their orders because of the excessive leadtimes. Half a year after the start of the large-scale ramp-up, company management decided it needed to start with a clean slate. Just before the end of the year, the company itself cancelled several months' worth of "difficult" orders. This is the peak in week 51 in Fig. 3.4. These existing orders were cancelled for a variety of reasons, ranging from data pollution to technical impediments or customer issues.

Already in December, the new order intake had been strongly reduced. Unfortunately, the fulfillment rate did not really pick up. In the next year, the order cancellation rate stayed significantly higher than the actual successful installs and the new order intake. So two outflows were going up,

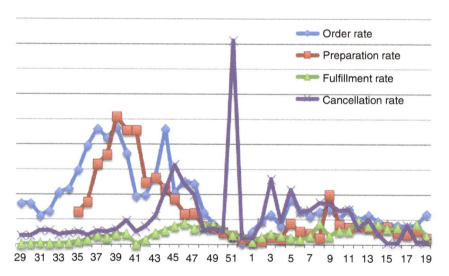

Fig. 3.4 Order flow rates during the large-scale ramp-up

and the inflow was going down. Collectively, these three flows gradually brought the fulfillment backlog down and the service supply chain back under control.

3.2   ROOT CAUSES: FACTORY PHYSICS AND MANAGERIAL MISPERCEPTIONS

What went wrong in this ramp-up? The root causes lie, on the one hand, with some fundamentals about the dynamics of service supply chains. One could even call these (*service) factory physics* (Hopp and Spearman 2000). On the other hand, managerial misperceptions are to blame. Of the following list of seven root causes, four really are factory physics. However, since management is mostly not aware of them, they could double as managerial misperceptions:

- Interconnected regulating feedback loops
- The rework cycle
- The Yerkes-Dodson Law
- Erosion of service quality
- The fallout effect
- The quality cascade
- Incorrect assumptions of scalability

The next pages will explain these mysterious labels.

Interconnected Regulating Feedback Loops

A service supply chain is a dynamic system and the behavior of any dynamics system is governed by a number of feedback loops, both positive, reinforcing ones and negative feedback loops. In the real world, there is never such a thing as a positive feedback loop *without* negative feedback loops. This is because positive feedback leads to exponential growth into infinity. And infinity is rare in social systems.

Figure 3.5 shows the key loops governing a generic service operations system. Because a positive feedback loop is so rare, there are both negative (balancing, denoted with a "B") and positive (regulating, denoted with an "R") feedback loops. None of these loops are active in the "steady state". In the steady state, all inflows equal the outflow for all the stocks in the system, so the net flow is zero.

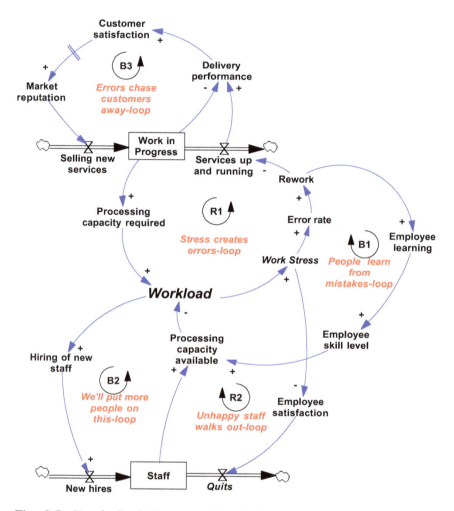

Fig. 3.5 Key feedback loops regulating behavior of a generic service system

So it all begins with the *inflow* of Selling new services becoming significantly higher than the *outflow* of Services up and running. When this happens, all five loops become active, but not all equally fast; the *delays* governing them will be different.

- *R1: Stress creates errors.* First the loop R1 will become visible. Higher workloads lead to more stress, which will lead to more errors (this is the Yerkes-Dodson Law, which we will discuss further on). More errors lead to lower productivity in order processing, and hence to even higher backlog and even higher workloads.
- *B2: We'll put more people on this.* A normal reaction from management is to add staff to alleviate such a persistent problem. That becomes problematic if there are no budgets, or if hiring and training delays are really long. Another version of this is to make staff work overtime. That will also lead to more employee hours, but and will also be quick to implement, but may lead to more burnout and hence over time boost two other reinforcing loops in the same system, loop R1 and loop R2.
- *R1: Unhappy staff walks out loop.* How quickly this loop will become effective is context-dependent. In the context of customer care centers where the average stay time is less than a year, this loop will become active quickly indeed. In the context of field technicians that on average spend decades with the same company, of course less so. However, another way of achieving the same effect is higher sick leave percentages. That too will decrease the staff effectively available. And that may start to have an effect within some weeks or months.
- *B1: People learn from mistakes.* Every cloud has a silver lining. From all this rework, staff will also learn, which will lead to higher employee skills, which will lead to more productivity, and so to more capacity, which will alleviate workloads and work stress, and so take off some steam from loop R1.
- *B3: Errors chase customers away.* Unfortunately for the company, a stakeholder outside of the jurisdiction of management governs an important regulating cycle: the customer. When it becomes clear that a service is not performing, such as in the case of the telco featured in this chapter, existing customers will cancel. New customer growth will become less. Typically, this is not the kind of regulation management prefers, but it will happen, nonetheless. How fast it will happen strongly depends on perception delays: how quickly will customer find out performance is bad. Often, an excessively long leadtime is a good proxy for customers to infer overall delivery performance (Forrester 1968).

The Rework Cycle

Every single order in this case really was a project in itself. Many different activities all had to be executed in a synchronized manner to activate one single customer. Unfortunately, many if not most projects cost more time and more money than anticipated. It is therefore not surprising that in this case it took far longer to activate customers than originally planned.

We know that, typically, projects do not finish in time. Partly, this is the result of the quality and workload-related delays described so far. Partly, projects are delays because of rework cycle effects (Cooper 1980). What are those?

The rework cycle in its generic form is shown in Fig. 3.6, adapted from Lyneis and Ford's (2007) overview article. The rework cycle includes four stocks of work. At the start of a project or project stage, all work resides in the stock "Original Work to Do". A fraction of the work being done at any point in time contains errors. Work done correctly enters the "Work Done" stock and never needs rework. However, work containing errors enters the "Undiscovered Rework" stock. These errors

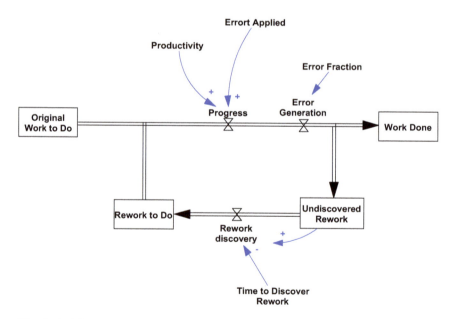

Fig. 3.6 The generic undiscovered rework cycle

are not immediately recognized, but are detected as a result of doing downstream work or testing.

This "Rework Discovery" may occur months or even years after the rework was created. Once discovered, the work moves to the backlog of "Rework to Do". Reworking an item can generate or reveal even more rework that must be done. Therefore, some reworked items flow through the rework cycle one or more subsequent times.

The effects of the rework cycle are huge. As summarized by Lyneis and Ford: "The rework cycle's recursive nature in which rework generates more rework that generates more rework, etc., creates problematic behaviors that often stretch out over most of a project's duration and are the source of many project management challenges" (ibid., p. 160).

The Yerkes-Dodson Law

When work has to be redone the workload increases. But when workload increases, errors will also increase. This effect was established in psychology over a century ago. Today it is known as the Yerkes-Dodson Law (Sterman 2000). It describes the relation between stress, or workload, and error rates, or quality. The effects of this law account for many of the productivity and feedback effects that also make projects take longer and cost more.

Yerkes and Dodson explored back in 1908 how performance in various tasks depends on the level of stress imposed. Low levels of arousal or stress actually yield low performance. Just think of the many car accidents that occur on long and boring rides. So, as stress, or in our formulation workload, increases, performance increases. However, there is a workload level at which stress no longer increases. So, the relation between workload and performance is an inverted U shape: low at the edges of very low and very high workload, optimal for a workload somewhere around 1.

Erosion of Service Quality

The challenge get bigger and bigger. It may even be so that management had become accustomed to lower service quality. This effect was captured in 2001 by Oliva and Sterman in a paper with the informative title: "Cutting corners and working overtime: Erosion of quality in the service industry". Again, this describes a vicious cycle. It starts with management that may bias service centers to reduce—albeit unintentionally—the level of service they provide to their customers. This can lock them into a vicious cycle of eroding service quality. Oliva and Sterman base their work on earlier case studies in the insurance industry (Senge 1990; Senge and Sterman 1992).

They formulate their theory as follows: Because of rising financial pressure driven by slow productivity growth, managers attempt to maximize throughput per employee and minimize expense ratios. Because it is relatively difficult to obtain productivity gains in high-contact services, maximizing throughput drives the employees to work harder and, eventually, to reduce the attention given to customers.

Obviously, this leads to lower-quality customer contacts. Employees cut corners to save time. Somewhere that will hurt quality. However, service quality and customer satisfaction are difficult to measure. What can be easily measured is time per customer spent. When that goes down, managers can easily interpret that as a productivity gain. That is also consistent with their objective of minimizing cost. The level of service consistent with cutting corners then becomes their new estimates of required service capacity.

In the longer run, the consequences of reducing attention to customer only grow: poor quality (e.g. rework), low customer loyalty, and high turnover of service personnel. Interpreted wrongly, this may even trigger more focus on cost control. This is again: *Focus on cost and quality goes down. Focus on quality and costs go down.*

The Fallout Effect

Semi-automated service supply chains are far more sensitive to variations in quality levels than manufacturing supply chains. Often the primary process step is fully automated or performed by customers themselves. In those settings, all the human capacity in the process is by definition dedicated to reworking those orders that require rework. Let's suppose that we have a quality level of 95%, so 5% of the orders fall out and have to be reworked for some reason or another (Fig. 3.7).

Let's say that there is a 10% increase in the *quantity* incoming order rate. How much additional capacity is needed then in order processing? Well, 0% more in the regular process, because that remains fully automated, but 10% more in the rework process, which is manual. Here, capacity appears to be proportionally related to the volume of work. However, what happens when there is a 5% decrease in *quality* while the

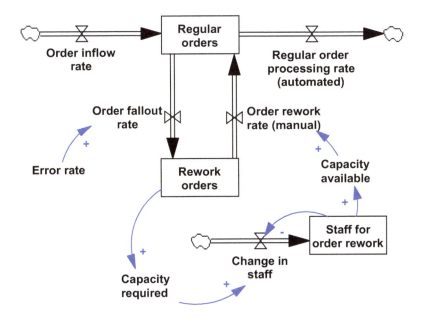

Fig. 3.7 Semi-automated order flow triggering the fallout effect

incoming order rate quantity remains the same? Then the amount of rework *doubles* from 5% to 10% of the order volume, and so the *required capacity increases with 100%*! This is the order fallout effect. Figure 3.8 gives an illustration from a case in a European telco where the Provisioning stage was a fully automated one, except for the handling of Provision fallout. Here capacity required in provisioning tripled as a result of order fallout.

Quality Cascades

Errors and queries cascade down the service supply chain. Contracting upstream is relatively easy. Moving downstream gets more and more difficult. Queries cascade back up again just as easily. When customers call the help desk, the help desk looks in the computer systems. But when those do not give immediate answers, this leads to an additional query, upstream, downstream, or both. When field technicians are faced with incorrect or incomplete order information, they call back. Meanwhile, addressing such

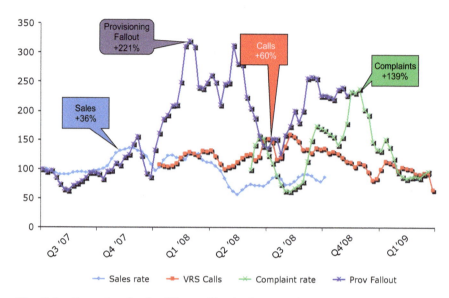

Fig. 3.8 Example of order fallout effect in the provisioning stage in the telecom service supply chain

queries costs time. That time cannot be spent on solving problems, or, even more importantly, on preventing them from happening in the first place. This is visualized in Fig. 3.9.

Nowadays, meetings and teleconference are a popular means of resolving issues. If you can't solve it on your own, let's organize a meeting. Part of these are useful, even essential. But in the context of intransparency and low quality, they first lead to even more time for talk and even less time for solving problems. In the end, it apparently takes management to cut the Gordian knot. In the case in this chapter, management simply throws out a third of the entire existing backlog just before the closing of the current budget year.

Limited Scalability

An important issue in service ramp-ups in IT-enabled services is scalability. Scalability can refer both to the service supply chain and to the service itself. It is the ability of a system, network, or process to handle a growing

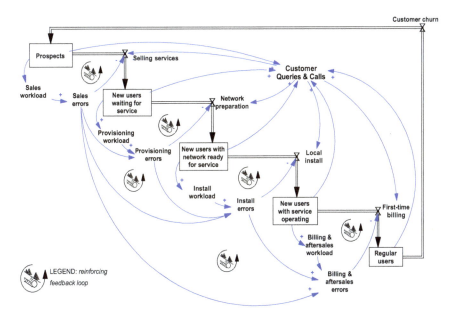

Fig. 3.9 A visualization of the quality cascade

amount of work in a capable manner or its ability to be enlarged to accommodate that growth. For the service itself, scalability is how it scales as it is deployed on larger systems and/or more systems or as more load is applied to it. Boyer et al. (2002) put forward a continuum from high to low scalability. Services that are pure information have high scalability; the more commoditized and standardized the service, the higher the scalability; the more unique the service and the more awkward the handling issues, the lower.

Management often incorrectly assumes infinite scalability in service operations, whereas there are always limitations, in particular in human capacity to deal with anomalies. The nursery room concept had worked fine because there were manual handovers everywhere. When the order rate was scaled up, this manual handover rate was simply not scalable.

To achieve high scalability firms seek to reduce their dependence on human resources though strategies such as automating customer support and overtly or covertly discouraging customers from interacting with employees. However, this can have severe limitations in two contexts.

First, when the physical component elements associated with such services do not lend themselves to high scalability. Examples include the size of the facilities investment and the logistics requirements (Boyer et al. 2002).

A second subtler limit to scalability is concerned with the complexity and predictability of the physical elements. Simple and predictable physical elements can be automated and easily scaled up. For example, when customer questions are highly predicable and dealing with them can be automated, but when complex or not predictable, the ability to automation and capacity needed are uncertain, and hence scalability is limited (Hallowell 2001). This was precisely what happened with the nursery room concept.

3.3   SYSTEMIC SOLUTIONS

Poka Yoke: *Avoid Errors*

The first systemic solution is to assure that quality is consistently high irrespective of the load on the system. *Poka Yoke* is the term introduced by Shigeo Shingo as part of the Toyota Production System method (Shingo 1989). *Poka* stands for "error", even "blunder", in Japanese, and *yoke* for "prevent, avoid". It deals with the prevention of errors, therefore. When there are no errors, there is nothing to cascade down the service supply chain. So, the goal should be to have consistently high quality. This is already difficult when demand is stationary; the challenge becomes much greater when demand is ramped up.

In the world of manufacturing, *Poka Yoke* has been developed into an elaborate set of techniques that are simple, visual, and widespread. Often they are failsafe, in the sense that there is just no other way of doing things than the right way. For example, a SIM card can only be inserted in a mobile phone the right way because one corner is cut off, which excludes all other non-correct ways of insertion.

In the world of services, and certainly of IT-enabled services, their use is much less widespread. Implicitly, the systemic solutions advocated in this book contain many of the Poka Yoke techniques such as "Ask five times why", "Go to the Gemba" (=factory floor), Cause and Effect/Ishikawa diagrams and Failure Mode, Effect, and Criticality Analysis (FMECA) (Shingo 1989; Womack et al. 1990; George 2003).

Eliminate Manual Workarounds

One translation of *Poka Yoke* to the world of IT-enabled services is to eliminate manual workarounds. Such workarounds are necessary when an order "falls out" from an automated process, such as happened in many of the cases in this book. As long as such manual workarounds remain necessary, one cannot ramp up to a tenfold of the current order rate, not even from 10 to a 100 per week, and certainly not from a 100 per week to a 1000 or more. Either one has to systematically eliminate these options for "fallout" or one has to live with them and ramp up more modestly.

Shorten Perception Delays

Sales continues to ramp up longer than the backoffice processes can sustain because it does not know how much load these can bear, not even how much their current load is. There is low transparency of downstream backlog, leadtimes, and workload. Suppose that this could be changed? Suppose it would be instantly clear when the system was being overloaded? What would happen then? Simulation modeling is a good way to investigate such a question. It can answer *What-if* questions without the need to execute them the real world.

A full description of the high-level simulation model that we will use next can be found in Akkermans et al. (2016). The purpose of this model was to broadly capture the dynamics of the case but especially to aid our intuition about what would be a sound policy from a systemic perspective. In the earlier figures, we saw that in this case there were really two ramp-ups, and also two ramp-downs. A small ramp-up during the nursery room phase and a big one from week 36 onwards, followed by a ramp-down toward the end of the year. The simulation model shows similar behavior, as can be seen in Fig. 3.10.

Why the ramp-up occurs seems logical, but why does the decision-making logic of the model decide on two occasions that it is time to ramp down? That becomes clearer from Fig. 3.11. This shows that as the ramp-up proceeds, backlog grows faster than capacity can grow. This leads to higher workload (not shown), which leads to more fallout and hence more rework, which further leads to high workload, and so on. Unfortunately, it takes sales some 2 months to notice that it has swamped the service supply chain.

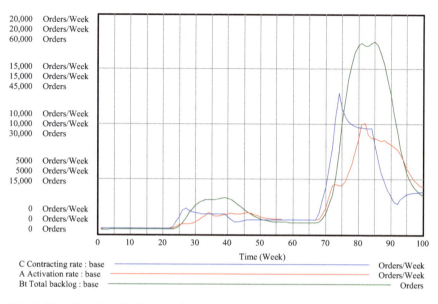

20,000	Orders/Week
20,000	Orders/Week
60,000	Orders
15,000	Orders/Week
15,000	Orders/Week
45,000	Orders
10,000	Orders/Week
10,000	Orders/Week
30,000	Orders
5000	Orders/Week
5000	Orders/Week
15,000	Orders
0	Orders/Week
0	Orders/Week
0	Orders

Time (Week)

C Contracting rate : base		Orders/Week
A Activation rate : base		Orders/Week
Bt Total backlog : base		Orders

Fig. 3.10   Simulated behavior of key supply chain variables in the ramp-up model

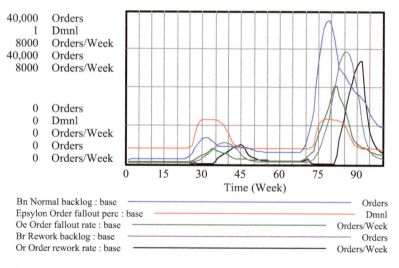

40,000	Orders
1	Dmnl
8000	Orders/Week
40,000	Orders
8000	Orders/Week
0	Orders
0	Dmnl
0	Orders/Week
0	Orders
0	Orders/Week

Time (Week)

Bn Normal backlog : base		Orders
Epsylon Order fallout perc : base		Dmnl
Oe Order fallout rate : base		Orders/Week
Br Rework backlog : base		Orders
Or Order rework rate : base		Orders/Week

Fig. 3.11   Simulated behavior of backlog, fallout, and rework

Sales sees that it has swamped the supply chain when its perception of the customer leadtime has become significantly higher than the desired leadtime. Leadtime is to be seen here as a proxy for delivery performance in general (Forrester 1968). What would happen if it would not take 8 weeks for Sales to perceive leadtimes, but just 1 week? This is the kind of What-if question that a simulation model is very helpful in. The results are shown in Figs. 3.12 and 3.13. Figure 3.11 shows the contracting ramp-up that is also shown in Fig. 3.10, albeit with a vastly different scale.

There are two key differences between the base case and the scenario with fast feedback on operational performance to sales. The first is the size of the feedback. The peaks now become fivefold of what they were under the base, which is very good from a revenue perspective. The second is the frequency of the ramp-up to ramp-down cycle. There are now four cycles in this 100-week timeframe. This creates far more volatility in both the frontoffice and the backoffice, which clearly is not desirable.

What is causing this very different behavior becomes evident from Fig. 3.13. This shows the performance in backoffice operational processes, *as perceived by Sales.* In the base case, this performance starts off as

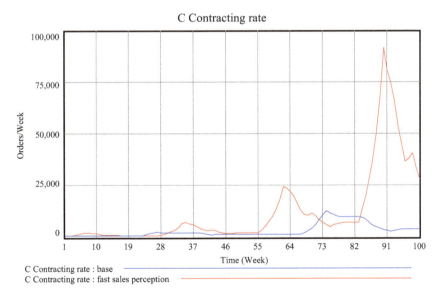

Fig. 3.12 Contracting ramp-up rates: base case versus fast ops feedback to sales

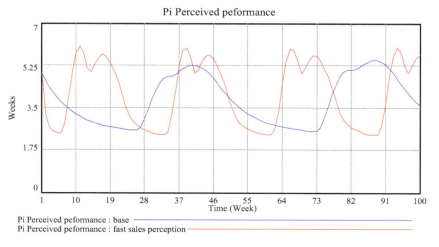

Pi Perceived peformance

Pi Perceived peformance : base ——————————
Pi Perceived peformance : fast sales perception ——————————

Fig. 3.13 Perception of operations performance by sales: base case versus fast feedback

satisfactory. [Satisfactory here is a value over 3.0.] At this time, the service is still under development. At around week 26, the service is ready for a ramp-up. This then continues until week 35, when performance is perceived as too low to continue the ramp-up. This takes until week 68, when performance is again deemed solid enough to ramp up once more.

When feedback to operations is much faster, this whole cycle also runs much faster. In total, four times can be completed within 2 years. These four ramp-ups lead to the resounding success in sales. And also to a success in operations, because the ramp-ups are stopped sooner. As a result, swamping of backoffice processes does not occur. So, this is a great policy. The next problem becomes, how such wonderful transparency of the myriad operational processes is to be achieved in practice.

Festina lente *in Service Ramp-Ups*

Perhaps it is smarter to go slower, rather than faster and faster. Already in 1995, Mass and Berkson noted that it is often better to "go slow to go fast" in volume ramp-ups. Their empirical setting was personal computer manufacturing, but this variation of *festina lente* appears just as true in services. Figure 3.14 shows the development of the installed base over time of another telecom service.

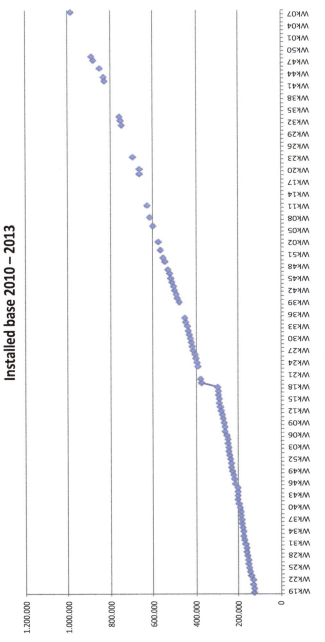

Fig. 3.14 Smooth ramp-up pattern for interactive TV services

Here, the lessons from earlier ramp-up disasters in the industry were really taken to heart. Within 5 years, this service had become the market leader in its region, despite fierce competition from various sources, with well over a million subscribers.

3.4   CONCLUSION

The pressure to ramp up new services can be immense. When all the managerial focus in the ramp-up is on managing the frontoffice processes, ramp-ups will go wrong. Synchronizing backoffice processes with frontoffice processes is essential if service ramp-ups are to go well. Backoffice processes are complex and often do not receive the attention they deserve. A whole series of complex dynamics can be triggered when sales rates grow faster than the capacity to deal with those orders can keep up. Better performance can be achieved when there is very good visibility of backoffice performance. However, this will happen at the expense of much more volatility. An alternative approach that appears more feasible and just as successful is to ramp up slowly, to "go slow to go fast". Again, here is an example of *festina lente* as a sound policy for service operations management.

REFERENCES

Akkermans, H., Voss, C., van Oers, R., & Zhu, Q. (2016, July). *Never the twain shall meet? Simulating Sales & Operations Planning ramp-up dynamics in IT-enabled service supply chains.* Proceedings International System Dynamics Conference, TU Delft. http://www.systemdynamics.org/conferences/2016/proceed/papers/P1314.pdf

Boyer, K., Hallowell, R., & Roth, A. (2002). E-services: Operating strategy—A case study and a method for analyzing operational benefits. *Journal of Operations Management, 20,* 175–188.

Cooper, K. G. (1980). Naval ship production: A claim settled and a framework built. *Interfaces, 10*(6), 20–36.

Forrester, J. W. (1968). Market growth as influenced by capital investment. *Industrial Management Review, 9*(2), 83–105.

George, M. L. (2003). *Lean six sigma for service.* New York: McGraw-Hill.

Hallowell, R. (2001). 'Scalability': The paradox of human resources in e-commerce. *International Journal of Service Industry Management, 12*(1), 34–43.

Hopp, W. J., & Spearman, M. L. (2000). *Factory physics* (2nd ed.). Boston: McGraw Hill.

Lyneis, J. M., & Ford, D. N. (2007). System dynamics applied to project management: A survey, assessment, and directions for future research. *System Dynamics Review, 23*, 157–189.

Mass, N., & Berkson, B. (1995). Going slow to go fast. *The McKinsey Quarterly, 4*, 19–29.

Oliva, R., & Sterman, J. D. (2001). Cutting corners and working overtime: Quality erosion in the service industry. *Management Science, 47*(7), 894–914.

Senge, P. (1990). *The fifth discipline: The art and practice of the learning organization.* New York: Doubleday.

Senge, P., & Sterman, J. (1992). Systems thinking and organizational learning: Acting locally and thinking globally in the organization of the future. *European Journal of Operational Research, 59*(1), 137–150.

Shingo, S. (1989). *A study of the Toyota production system from industrial engineering viewpoint.* New York: Productivity Press.

Sterman, J. D. (2000). *Business dynamics: Systems thinking and modeling for a complex world.* New York: McGraw-Hill.

Womack, J. P., Jones, D. T., & Roos, D. (1990). *The machine that change the world.* New York: Harper Collins.

CHAPTER 4

Customer Interactions: *How to Enrage Customers with a Great Service*

Abstract Sometimes a great new service actually enrages customers, simply because its service operations are not managed properly. In this age of social media, customer outrage can happen much more frequently and get out of control much sooner. In this chapter we look at what happens when interaction with the customer base gets completely out of control. We investigate a case of a very successful service that provided great quality at very reduced prices to customers but that still led to a national outrage. Senior management found itself forced to appear on national TV on consumer programs in front of audiences full of enraged and deeply frustrated customers of this new service. They felt they were truly very unlucky. Or could they have seen this coming?

Sometimes a great new service actually enrages customers, simply because its service operations are not managed properly. In this age of social media, customer outrage can happen much more frequently and get out of control much sooner. In this chapter we look at what happens when interaction with the customer base gets completely out of control. We investigate a case of a very successful service that provided great quality at very reduced prices to customers but that still led to a national outrage. Senior management found itself forced to appear on national TV on consumer

© The Author(s) 2018   55
H. Akkermans, *Service Operations Dynamics*,
https://doi.org/10.1007/978-3-319-72017-3_4

programs in front of audiences full of enraged and deeply frustrated customers of this new service. They felt they were truly very unlucky. Or was this not bad luck? Could they have seen this coming?

4.1   NOT QUITE THE MEDIA ATTENTION WE WANTED

In this part of Europe where this case is set, the telecom market for fixed line services is split evenly between the coax cable of the cable companies and the copper wire (or, increasingly, glass fiber) of the telcos, of which the company in this case was the biggest operator. Back in 2005, top management took a bold decision. It was faced with an ever-increasing rate of what is called "line loss". The number of subscribers for its traditional, fixed line telephony services declined. This was because other telecom operators offered similar services more cheaply and cable companies were moving from their traditional market of TV signals to telephony services as well. Most importantly, after several years of haggling over standards and technology, telephony over the Internet, called VoIP (Voice over Internet Protocol), was taking off as a viable telecom service to consumers.

Then, top management decided not to wait for the inevitable to happen but to start cannibalizing its own existing base of traditional telephony customers with a homegrown version of VoIP. The announcement to the investment community and to the press of VoIP services offered came in the middle of 2005, but it took several months before the service could be offered to significant numbers of customers.

Very Successful Service, Very Fast Ramp-Up

At first, the ordering and installing of VoIP was tested with a small number of friendly users, up to a few hundred new orders per week. Then, finally, the day arrived that "everybody" could order this new product. Rather unexpectedly, almost everybody did. One manager responsible for the original rollout of VoIP recalls that at the end of the first day that VoIP orders could be placed, some 12,000 orders appeared in the order entry systems. Originally, the order intake for this new service had been dimensioned at 500 new orders per week. Apparently, employees in the retail shops owned by the telco had been saving up orders from people who had heard of the new service and had placed these on waitlists. On that first day, they put the order data for all these early adopters into the order management systems. So from the first day of its commercial existence, the VoIP service supply chain was swamped.

After a few months, things stabilized. New people were hired, and further fixes were made in the patchwork of non- or partly automated process steps that together made up the VoIP service chain. The success story continued.

Top management immediately noticed the huge commercial success of this new offering. Figure 4.1 shows the demand pattern for VoIP for Q1 2006 up to Q3 2007. From this picture, it becomes clear that in the second half of 2006, demand for VoIP exploded. Unheard-of numbers of customers ordered VoIP and the broadband access that went with it, which was great for the company's market share in broadband services. At the end of 2006, there were half a million VoIP users which was almost just as much as the number of customers that had cancelled their traditional telephone service, so the feared exodus of customers had been prevented.

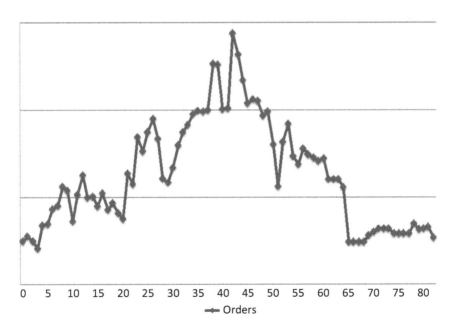

Fig. 4.1   Orders for VoIP, Q1 2006—Q3 2007, normalized

Gradual Escalation of Issues

Internally, issues were mounting. There was simply not enough capacity in the service supply chain to connect all these new customers in time. Even less capacity to serve the fast-growing installed base. Leave alone the capacity needed to deal with technical issues that popped up in this new innovative service. Next to staffing, there were several technical bottlenecks as well. There were technical bottlenecks for new customers. For instance, when they would activate the service in their home, they needed to gain access to the total network. In order to do so, they needed to pass a certain server that turned out not to be dimensioned properly. It simply could not deal with so many customers at one time. As a result, activation would fail. This would result in calls to the help desk from customers, and to calls from the field engineers to the backoffice. That would result in even more attempts to gain access, more delays, and so on.

Also, the fast-growing installed base of customers suffered from growing technical issues. All customers needed a modem in their homes, a so-called RG, "Residential Gateway". Some distance away from the bloodshed in the trenches of VoIP, purchasing management had decided that a new RG was needed from a new supplier, to reduce the company's dependency on its current supplier. For this new RG to work properly, the chain needed a new communication protocol for IP telephony. This new protocol was basically a software program that had to be downloaded to all the RGs in the chain, both new and old ones.

The new RG needed to be rushed into operation because the old types were running out of stock quicker than expected. As a result, there were still some flaws in the protocol software. When this new software had been "rolled out" to the entire VoIP customer base, this resulted in errors in telephone traffic for all users of VoIP, not just the new ones. These errors resulted in a flood of work for the service staff. After all, even a small percentage of a big number is a large number. Say you are receiving 10,000 new orders per week and your installed base is 100,000. Then, an increase of only 10% of errors from your installed base doubles the incoming order rate for your service staff.

Public Outrage

By December, there was a public outrage. An extended quote from a national consumer program from December 2006 is illustrative:

Never before did we receive so many complaints in such a short time about a product. In September we already reported on VoIP. Back then we already received hundreds of complaints, but the flow kept growing. Therefore we again focus on this new service. (…)

Here is a listing of the complaints we received. The helpdesk is hard to reach, you are on hold a long time. A promise is made that you will be called back but often that does not happen. (…) When there is just a small thing wrong with a connection it can take months before you can use VoIP. Then there is the category malfunctioning. Not being able to call, not being able to receive calls, no Internet access, these complaints we often encounter.

In September we asked the company to stop sales promotions, but the company says that the large majority is satisfied and that percentagewise, complaints are not that many. They have thousands of new customers every week, which is why they do not see the need for a stop in sales activity.

The company's reaction to the consumer program was illustrative as well:

Partly, the complaints are caused by the huge demand. VoIP is an enormously popular service, we can say the most popular in the country. We activate every week thousands of customers and thousands of customers install the service themselves every week. The totals imply that a medium-sized town is connected every week. It is for us unacceptable that our customers still have problems with the install, but this does indicate that it will take us some more time to resolve all issues.

Clearly, this was not enough. Hardboiled top managers at the company still recall the public flogging they received on national TV. In front of a studio audience of outraged customers their comments about "percentagewise a small number" did not go down well at all. Clearly, they had not realized how high emotions could rise. For them, this was just a service with some technical issues. For the people in the audience, this was about basic social functions such as communicating via mail or phone and a company that clearly wasn't interested in helping them.

Complete Shutdown

Early February 2007, top management finally took the inevitable decision. It publically announced that it would no longer be promoting sales of the new service. It would first try to fix problems with existing customers. A leading newspaper reported:

[TELCO] HITS THE BRAKES ON INTERNET TELEPHONY
[Telco] has stopped promoting its VoIP services. The telecom company first wants to clear the large pile of complaints with its subscribers.

The company could not deal with the inflow of new VoIP customers last year. It received over half a million VoIP customers. At the peak, some 20,000 new customers were noted. In around 5% of the cases complex problems occurred.

"That is an unacceptable level," [the CEO] said, in a press meeting for the annual results. Still thousands of customers are waiting for a working Internet connection. "We have become the victims of our own success."

There are two words that are especially noteworthy in this text. The first one is *complex*. So, 5% of the orders led to complex problems. That means that a significantly higher percentage had problems? It probably does; 5% of 500,000 is 25,000 customers with serious problems. That is indeed a small European town full. The other noteworthy word is *victims*. Apparently, company management felt it had not done anything wrong. It was just bad luck that had hit them. They were the real victims, not those 25,000+ customers?

4.2   Root Causes: New Realities and Old Misconceptions

The root causes for this disaster are multiple. Some are new; most are rather old. Again, they are either technical and operational or managerial and perceptional, or both. Several of these root causes appear in multiple places in this book.

- Social media effects of customer backlogs;
- Intransparency of quality issues.
- Managerial sensemaking delays.
- Inadequate supply chain control.
- Misaligned managerial incentives.

Social Media Effects of Customer Backlogs

In 2006, social media were not yet as big as they are today. Their propensity to escalate issues to huge proportions was less known than it is today. Discussions on social media undeniably played a part in the public outrage.

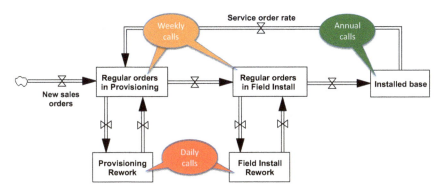

Fig. 4.2 Frequency of calling depending on customer status

But they were not the decisive factor. Much more important was that huge backlog of tens of thousands of customers with issues that were not resolved. Why?

It is easy to blame social media for the public outrage, but the root cause for that outrage is the backlog of customers with problems that became too large. Why? Because customers that have problems keep calling. Every day, if they must. One internal study suggested that such customers would call on average some 17 times before from the beginning of their problems until these were finally resolved.

Figure 4.2 explains the massive impact of a small number of customers with problems. It shows that existing customers in the installed base will typically call 1–1.5 times per year. New customers whose orders don't have major issues will get activated in just a few weeks, and they may call every week. However, customers whose orders that are in rework, be it still in the provisioning stage at the telco or already in field install at the customer site, will call *every day*. They cannot use the phone and they cannot use the Internet, which is almost as much a utility as electricity and running water. One year later, the duration of the problem still mostly drove the number of calls, as is evident from an analysis made of call ratio drivers shown in Fig. 4.3.

Mostly, these frustrated customers will call the telco, and that will create great stress on frontoffice and backoffice processes, as we saw in the previous chapter. But they will also want to vent their anger and frustration to others via social media. And when there are many thousands of those, they will create a true media storm.

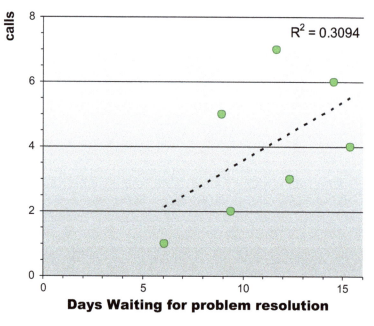

Fig. 4.3 Analysis of call ratio drivers in VoIP chain, June 2008

Intransparency of Quality Issues

Management underestimated the size of the quality issues, perhaps also because they did not fully appreciate the complexity of the operational tasks that needed to be executed and perhaps also because the commercial success blinded them. The minutes from a management team meeting of the Fixed Line Division in September tells the story. Yes, there is reference to the operational issues: "trends in complaints extremely disturbing". Especially since "costs are exploding". However, mostly there was cause for celebration, because "in August X number of VoIP have been sold, which is an outstanding performance (and a record!)".

Meanwhile, the operational issues had been growing long after sales revenue had begun to slow down. Complaints (so, angry customers), and staff (so, costs) kept growing. In retrospect, telco management estimates that this ramp-up cost them some 100 million euros more than originally budgeted.

Managerial Sensemaking Delays

Management simply took too long to make sense of the situation it had gotten into. Reducing the inflow of new orders would have been a very good idea in the summer of 2006. Instead, the company took this painful decision half a year and tens of millions of avoidable costs later. Why was that? There has been much research on what is called managerial sensemaking (Weick 1995, 2001), on managerial decision filters (Russo et al. 2008), and on decision traps (Russo and Schoemaker 1989; van Oorschot et al. 2013) and Fig. 4.4 is an attempt to arrive at a synthesis of these insights.

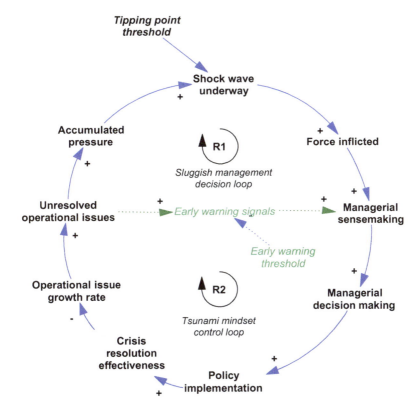

Fig. 4.4 The managerial decision cycle for business tsunami. (Adapted from Akkermans and Van Wassenhove 2018)

Events such as the failed introduction of VoIP are so-called business tsunami: major events that happen rarely but that change a company's supply chain practices for good, if they do not destroy the company right away. The logic in Fig. 4.4 largely follows the logic of an ecological tsunami as much as it mimics the logic of a business tsunami. At the top of the diagram, the tipping point is passed. For earthquakes, this happens when tectonic plate pressures generate more strain than local rock "elasticity" can bear (Grotzinger and Jordan 2014). For business tsunamis, it occurs when pressures in the environment become too big to contain. In the case of VoIP, this was the national outrage.

The top left of the diagram shows how those pressures built up over time. Moving counterclockwise one more step reveals a key difference between an ocean and business tsunami: companies can stop the buildup of pressures in their internal supply chain. External pressures almost brought the company and its service supply chain down. However, their origins lay internally, in operational supply chain issues that were too long ignored.

Inadequate Supply Chain Control

In the spring of 2007, the author facilitated a number of workshops with over 100 company staff to learn the lessons from this crisis. From these, it became painstakingly clear that this service supply chain was never designed to handle so many customers. Rather than having been designed for a specific purpose, it had grown organically. As a result, lots of inefficiencies still existed and lots of checks and balances were missing. When it was put under pressure, this service supply chain got out of control, at every level.

- At the operational level, the control mode was crisis management.
- At the tactical level, the organization was strongly stovepiped. Integral responsibility was lacking.
- At the strategic level, the service supply chain was grown, not built. Nobody had an overview of the entire chain.

Misaligned Managerial Incentives

Every part of the service supply chain had its own responsibilities and targets and acted accordingly. This led to a completely misaligned service supply chain. Operations was not willing to invest beforehand, in anticipation of the customer order increase projected by Sales. Sales was not willing to listen to the complaints from Operations about technical issues with customers and associated capacity limitations. Purchasing was not focused on buying error-free equipment, only on getting the cheapest. IT was focusing on service level agreements (SLAs) per box, not on a reliable end-to-end support of the business processes. In a guest lecture some years later, one top manager summarized the organizational setup at this time as follows:

- *Extreme compartmentalization*:
  - *Highly technology-oriented*
  - *History of product/service stovepipes*
  - *Traumatized by financial crisis*
  - *Management focus and incentives still on fragmented P&L* [=Profit & Loss Statements]
  - *Vain drive to decomplex by compartmentalization*
- *Crisis management mentality: fighting symptoms*
- *Push on Sales to grow revenue*

  - *Line loss issues*
  - *Extreme competitive pressure*
- *Shrinking product lifetimes*

In summary, the VoIP crisis was not a result of some really bad luck; it was an accident that had been waiting to happen. The company really needed to find some structural and systemic solutions for its problems or such crises would happen again.

4.3   Systemic Solutions

The company needed to change at three different levels.

- Firstly, it needed to really design and test its service supply chains.
- Secondly, it had to install a business process that would manage these supply chains from an integral perspective.
- And, thirdly, it had to develop a different mindset, one that was constantly on the lookout for early warning signals for unlikely events with high impact.

Design and Test-Drive the Service Supply Chain

After the sales drive had stopped, the hard work of fixing the problems started. At the beginning of 2006, some of the senior managers at KPN Telecom that were managing this crisis requested the development of a system dynamics model to arrive at a root cause understanding of the issues. As a result, some one hundred twenty managers and employees from KPN took part in four big group-model-building workshops facilitated by the author.

The mapping technique used in those workshops was causal loop diagramming and stocks and flow diagramming (Sterman 2000), which are specific modeling techniques. However, much of what happened here resonates with what Shapiro et al. wrote in 1992 about what needs to be done to fix order management cycles in general. "Draw your order management cycle and chart the gaps. (…) graphically chart (…) the order flow from the first step to the last, highlighting problem, opportunities and potential action steps. (…) This visual tool made it possible for different people from different functions and levels in the organization to (…) discuss the order flow with a clear and shared picture in front of them. (…) the chart guaranteed that disagreements over problems would focus on facts rather than on opinions" (Shapiro et al. 1992, p. 120).

In this series of workshops both backoffice and frontoffice staff were presented, from sales to billing, but also members of the board. To all involved it became clear that this service supply chain had grown organically, it had not been designed from the start. As an obvious consequence, its performance under stress had never been tested, such as would have been normal for any technical design. Therefore, a simulation model was developed from the mapping exercise to perform a "stress test" on suggested improvements to the service supply chain.

In April 2007 the key insights of this modeling exercise were presented to top management. The top message was that interactions of order quantity and quality had led to vicious cycles of bad performance. Several policy scenarios were evaluated:

- What if we ramp up again to a steady 15,000 orders per week? Stabilization over time will occur, but at a fairly high cost level to deal with all the queries and rework.
- What if we again have a technology bottleneck for new customer access to the network? Damage would occur again, but the by now big installed base would not be affected.

- What if we have a performance issue for the installed base? A very costly affair, due to the size of the installed base.
- What if we focus on acquiring "simple" customer sites? Marginal effects.
- What if we offer free field technicians to aid in installing? Shorter leadtimes, but the regular service process for the growing installed base will drain most capacity.

All these were questions that had been voiced repeatedly but for which there were no clear answers. Now those answers could be given. Now management had a model that could handle all the complexities simultaneously. And this model was credible, as it had been developed based on the input of some one hundred key staff.

The presentation ended with a cartoon of which the CTO (Chief Technical Officer) said afterward that it had helped him understand the essence of the issue better than all the sophisticated graphs up to that point.

Figure 4.5 shows that with higher quality as a lever, the company would be needing far less capacity to serve a growing installed base. In this

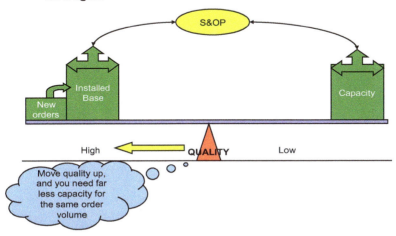

Fig. 4.5 Summarizing cartoon from presenation to top management at the end of project

analogy of a seesaw the logic was simple and compelling enough, but in the complexity of daily reality it was not. A decade later, the seesaw metaphor made it to the cover of this book.

Integral Sales & Operations Planning

As a direct result of this crisis and the lessons learned, the company set up Sales & Operations Planning (S&OP) processes for all its major services in the years that followed. It became the standard way of working for a number of years. These were regular meetings where functional units would inform each other of present status and plans for the near future, and where current problems could be discussed.

Unfortunately, what these S&OP meetings could still not do is translate capacity requirements from one part of the service supply chain to another. Without an integrated simulation model, management could still not "test-drive" the service supply chain.

Searching for the Gray Swans

So, here's the question: Would Telco's management have stopped their successful service ramp up sooner if they had had clearer reports on the size of the rework pool of customer orders?

Perhaps the following is safe to say. Without full visibility on supply chain developments, management is blind and accidents will happen. With supply chain visibility in the ordinary sense of the word, management may not see far or deep enough to spot a business tsunami in the making. Even with deep visibility, only a mindset that is actively on the lookout for rare events that run counter to conventional wisdom will catch such signals in time (Weick 1995, 2001; Akkermans and Van Wassenhove 2018).

After all, we live in interesting times. From 9/11 to the credit crisis, from the Japanese tsunami to Hurricane Sandy, but also from the iPhone to Facebook, this is the age of highly nonlinear events. In the words of Nassim Taleb, the author of the influential *The Black Swan* (2007), we have moved to Extremistan, "where inequalities are such that one single observation can disproportionately impact the aggregate" (Taleb 2007, p.33).

Demand for a hot new product, for example, in short lifecycle electronic equipment, no longer rises with 10% or 20% per month, but can rise with 100%. However, demand for new services such as VoIP can easily grow with 1000% or 2000%. The waves are an order of magnitude higher than anything we have seen before. And most of these highly nonlinear events, both the disasters and the desirable ones, are also highly unlikely. They are usually the combination of two or more very unlikely events taking place at precisely the same time.

Most if not all service supply chain tsunami are foreseeable and therefore manageable. They result from *gray swan events*, which are in themselves rare and unlikely events, but they are not unique: similar events have occurred repeatedly in the past. They may by now be forgotten, or underestimated, or ignored, or even shoved under the table for the time being by management (Taleb 2007; Akkermans and van Wassenhove 2013). However, every 5 years or every decade they will occur again. The wild amplification effects from the telco in 1995 described in Chap. 2 were not all so different from what happened again in 2006 in the current chapter. Telecom industry veterans recalled that in the first years of the new century, the introduction of DSL, so high-speed Internet connections, caused similar problems.

4.4   Conclusion

Introducing a wonderful new service that customers love and that still generates a national outrage sounds like really bad luck. However, as this chapter has shown, it was rather an incident waiting to happen. The service supply chain was not designed to deal with such large volumes of new customers. The product was not sufficiently mature so that order fulfillment issues could be prevented. Supply chain control was completely lacking as all parts of the chain were optimizing their own functional silos. For a long time, pressures within the company and within the customer base were building up, ignored, or underestimated by management. When those pressures passed a tipping point, a tsunami of customer complaints was unavoidable. Again, management of this service company would have done better by combining haste with moderation, or, as the Ancients would say: *festina lente.*

References

Akkermans, H. A., & van Wassenhove, L. N. (2013). Searching for the grey swans: The next 50 years of production research. *International Journal of Production Research, 51*(23–24), 6746–6755.

Akkermans, H. A., & van Wassenhove, L. N. (2018). A dynamic model of managerial response to grey swan events in supply networks. *International Journal of Production Research*, published online October 31, 2017, forthcoming in print.

Grotzinger, J. P., & Jordan, T. H. (2014). *Understanding earth*. New York: W.H. Freeman.

Russo, J. E., & Schoemaker, P. J. H. (1989). *Decision traps: The ten barriers to brilliant decision making and how to overcome them*. New York: Simon & Schuster.

Russo, J. E., Carlson, K. A., Meloy, M. G., & Yong, K. (2008). The goal of consistency as a cause of information distortion. *Journal of Experimental Psychology: General, 137*, 456–470.

Shapiro, B. P., Rangan, V. K., & Sviokla, J. J. (1992, July–August). Staple yourself to an order. *Harvard Business Review, 70*, 113–122.

Sterman, J. D. (2000). *Business dynamics: Systems thinking and modeling for a complex world*. New York: McGraw-Hill.

Taleb, N. N. (2007). *The black swan. The impact of the highly improbable*. New York: Random House.

Van Oorschot, K. E., Akkermans, H. A., Sengupta, K., & Van Wassenhove, L. N. (2013). Anatomy of a decision trap in complex new product development projects. *Academy of Management Journal, 56*(1), 285–307.

Weick, K. E. (1995). *Sensemaking in organizations*. Thousand Oaks: Sage.

Weick, K. E. (2001). *Making sense of the organization*. Malden: Blackwell.

CHAPTER 5

Managing Workforce Dynamics: *Hiring with Moderation*

Abstract The most important stakeholder after your customer base is your workforce. Here too, important dynamics can occur in service operations. In this chapter we zoom in on those, based on the case study of a Dutch legal aid insurance service. When the company's parent company, a retail bank, began selling insurance bundles, the company's number of insurance holders doubled in a few years. However, so did the demand for legal aid. Workforce growth lagged behind greatly. Soon, a huge backlog of pending requests formed. How should management then respond? At full speed or with moderation? The chapter includes a system dynamics analysis of the dynamic interactions between workforce numbers, learning curves, case backlog, customer and employee satisfaction, outsourcing, and costs. This analysis identified several high-leverage policies.

The most important stakeholder after your customer base is your workforce. Here too, important dynamics can occur in service operations. In this chapter we zoom in on those.

5.1   MORE WORK THAN ANTICIPATED

The case study described in this chapter (Akkermans and van Oorschot 2005) concerned a business unit of one of the leading insurers in the Netherlands. In 2003, the company employed some 6000 people and its

H. Akkermans, *Service Operations Dynamics*,
https://doi.org/10.1007/978-3-319-72017-3_5

revenues were 5 billion euros. The business unit concerned was called "Foundation for Legal Aid" (abbreviated from here on as "FLA"). In 2006, some 600,000 consumers had insured themselves for judicial aid with this formally independent organization. Some 300 FLA employees provided this legal aid.

A Very Successful New Service Offering

When demand for your service doubles, capacity of your staff will need to double as well, in headcount, in productivity, or in both. What FLA management in 2000 had not realized was that it was certain that the demand for its services would increase significantly, albeit with a long delay. The parent company, a retail bank, had begun a policy of selling bundles of insurances, in which there was also an option for legal aid insurance. This was a very successful commercial policy, and as a result FLA's number of insurance holders grew rapidly. Moreover, this took place in an era where people were more and more inclined to resolve issues using formal legal means. The inevitable consequence of this was that demand for legal aid increased for several years with an average of some 15%, as Fig. 5.1 shows.

Long Leadtimes, Huge Backlog of Work

When demand rises faster than capacity can keep up, huge backlog and leadtimes are inevitable. This also happened with this insurance company.

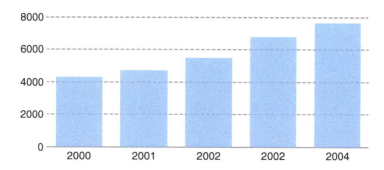

Fig. 5.1 Growth in inflow of new requests for legal aid, 2000–2004

Long leadtimes mean high work pressure for employees and poor service to clients. Apparently, the original management team (MT) was not able to cope with these growth problems, because when the author started to work with this company as a consultant, almost all MT members, including the Director, were less than a year in their current job.

Discontent with Customers, Staff, and Managers

There is no real trade-off between dissatisfied customers, employees, or managers. In the long run, they can only be dissatisfied or satisfied. And, indeed, at this time, there was discontent all around. Customers were dissatisfied, since their cases took too long to resolve and staff was often too busy to respond promptly to their questions. Staff was also dissatisfied, because they had too much work on their plate. At this time, a reorganization was being implemented that, over time, had to make their work more productive, but that started with disrupting their work routines.

Management was also unhappy. Not just because of the discontent with these two stakeholders, but also because they found it difficult to figure out what best to do. Staff was being hired, of course, but experienced staff was also leaving the company. Moreover, a shift from a regional organization to an organization per legal specialism had been implemented, but was that going well? For the time being, things only seemed to be getting worse, not better. Meanwhile, management had over a hundred performance indicators to look at. That was not only far too much to keep track of, but it also resulted in inconsistent messages.

5.2   ROOT CAUSES

Again in this chapter we see a combination of "factory physics", cognitive biases, and feedback loops interconnecting these. More specifically, the key root causes that come to mind here are the following.

- Long backlog depletion delays
- Long hiring and training delays
- Long managerial perception delays
- Lack of operational orientation with management

- Non-consumer-oriented professional orientation of staff
- Lack of managerial focus and coordination
- Multiple interconnected workforce-related feedback loops

The first two are more of the factory physics category, the next four are more behavioral, and the last one is the truly systemic one.

Long Backlog Depletion Delays

It is inevitable that when backlog has been building up for over a year that it cannot be depleted within a few weeks or months. Having a yearly increase in inflow of 15% means that the outflow also has to grow by 15%. If the outflow is less, it means that the backlog grows. If this has been less for several years, it means that the backlog has become really big. In Chap. 2 we saw an example where management depleted the backlog by simply cancelling a third of the orders, but here that was not an option.

Long Hiring and Training Delays

It is equally inevitable that qualified service employees take a long time to hire and a long time to train. In this case, the legal experts needed were also much in demand in the job market. This is a specific, almost niche area of the legal profession. So, it takes practice to become fully productive in it.

Long Managerial Perception Delays

What remains strange is that management of FLA was confronted with almost twice as many insurance holders and still somehow did not expect that it would have to deal with twice as many requests for legal aid. When management finally saw that the problems had become big, they did not sufficiently realize what were the right levers to pull either. Had a higher hiring rate started as soon as the client base began to grow, there would not have been a crisis.

Lack of Operational Orientation with Management

The original MT was not focused on running this unit like a factory, on balancing supply and demand. In the words of the new Director, there was "no thinking about improving processes". That meant that every 15% increase in the number of cases could only be dealt with 15% more staff. However, capacity available, in terms of cases that can be handled per period, is by definition equal to the product of the number of staff and their productivity. When you do not improve processes, you lose out on the opportunity to improve productivity. And with 15% more productivity and 0% more staff, capacity available is also equal to capacity required.

Non-Consumer-Oriented Professional Orientation

The work ethic of a professional lawyer leads to very different choices than customers may want. As the Director summarized: "Quality of legal work was the only driver." Now it may seem that this is something clients should be happy with but it often isn't. Often, clients prefer a quick settlement over a lengthy and uncertain court procedure that perhaps gets them a slightly better deal after a long period of uncertainty and agony. Needless to say, a quick settlement increases staff productivity a great deal at the same time as well.

Lack of Managerial Focus and Direction

Management was paralyzed by all the things it should and could monitor. At the time the author started to work with the company, management attempted to monitor performance from a list of over 130 performance indicators. From a perspective of bounded rationality (Simon 1957), it is not surprising that they were swamped. It has long been known that rationality of human decision making is best described as "bounded", rather than optimal (Cyert and March 1963). This is caused by cognitive limitations to knowledge. Psychology has long established that for most humans short-term working memory is limited too "7±2" chunks of information (Miller 1956).

Moreover, partly as a result of this, management failed to see the causal interconnections between the various performance elements. They could not see clear priorities in this large set of key performance indicators (KPIs).

Multiple Interconnected Workforce-Related Feedback Loops

In this case of professional services, the workforce plays a central role in many of the regulating feedback loops. This becomes apparent from the

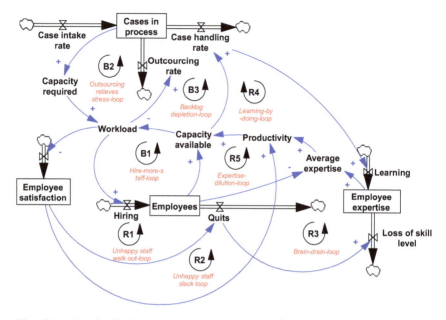

Fig. 5.2 Key feedback loops in workforce interactions

stocks-and-flows diagram in Fig. 5.2, which contains eight loops, all connected to the workforce.

- *B1: Hire more staff loop.* The first thing that happened in response to the increase in work is that more staff was hired. This was not sufficient to bring workloads to acceptable levels, so reinforcing feedback loops R1 and R2 remained active.
- *R1: Unhappy staff walks out loop.* The external job market for lawyers was good at this time, FLA had good qualified staff, and the organizational changes alone might make a highly qualified legal expert quite unhappy, apart from the work pressure.
- *R2: Unhappy staff slack loop.* This means that unhappy staff will be less productive. For instance, at the start of the reorganization, sick leave rate was at 9%. In subsequent years this went back to 5%. This further increased workloads, making the remaining staff even more unhappy, and so on.

- *R3: Brain drain loop.* When experienced staff leaves, this further reduces the available expertise, which lowers average productivity: the "brain drain" loop. All these three effects only aggravate the capacity issues.
- *B2: Outsourcing relieves stress loop.* The company had begun to experiment with outsourcing some of the work, which helped to let off steam and mitigate some of the workload effects. However, the costs of doing so appeared prohibitive.
- *R4: Learning by doing loop.* Meanwhile, staff, especially new staff, continued to learn from the processing of cases and got better and more productive at it. This was a slow process, however, that did not show strong results in the short run (but did in the longer run).
- *R5. Experience dilution loop.* The learning on the job was outweighed by another effect occurring simultaneously: as more new staff joined, staff who were new and inexperienced, the average expertise level was "diluted". Here is a numerical example of why that is: When 50 new staff with 0 years of experience join a group of 100 with 15 years' experience, the average experience will by definition drop 5 years. Average experience = Total years of experience/Total workforce = $(0 * 50 + 100 * 15) / (100 + 50) = 10$.
- *B3: Backlog depletion loop.* Only when there were more cases being handled per month than there were new ones arriving did the backlog start to shrink. When that happens, no more staff is needed, in principle. But an overshoot of staff is quite likely, as we will see in the next section.

5.3   SYSTEMIC SOLUTIONS: ASSURING RELEVANCE

The case study in this chapter is a happy study, since the changes initiated by management were very successful. Indeed, the approach chosen was a highly systemic one, with (1) first developing a conceptual integral perspective, then (2) testing it with a quantified model, (3) learning the key insights from the modeling, and (4–6) then implementing these in a number of specific operational improvements:

1. An integral Balanced Score Card (BSC) perspective
2. Simulation modeling to "assure relevance"
3. Accept worse-before-better performance
4. Outsourcing as a pressure valve

5. Changing workflows and mindsets
6. Hire with moderation

An Integral Balanced Score Card (BSC) Perspective

Management developed a BSC to obtain focus and consistency in its policy. This development took place via a systemic analysis of key company goals, business processes, performance indicators, and interactions between these. This systemic analysis took the form of a joined model and BSC development (Akkermans and van Oorschot 2005).

Model/score card development was set up in two stages. During the first stage, preparatory interviews were conducted with MT members, the results of which were discussed in a half-day workshop where the group engaged in a number of causal loop diagramming exercises. The findings from this workshop were summarized in a so-called workbook (Vennix 1996), which was distributed to the MT members, studied, filled in, and sent back.

This causal diagram was then again discussed in a full-day workshop. On the basis of these discussions, the first version of a BSC was generated. MT members could choose key indicators from the diagram that they felt would enable management to have a good grasp of the key drivers of performance. The initial set of selected performance indicators was discussed, refined, simplified, and finally agreed upon. The intermediate version of the BSC that formed the end result of this day is shown in Table 5.1.

Perhaps the most important managerial insight that emerged from this stage was that management came to realize how goals that they had first believed to be at odds with each other were, in fact, not mutually exclusive but mutually reinforcing. It was not choose for customer satisfaction *or* for employee satisfaction or for cost effectiveness, but rather we will achieve either *all* three goals or none at all. The key linking concept was productivity. Higher productivity does mean greater cost effectiveness, but also greater customer satisfaction as cases are handled sooner and with greater employee satisfaction as work pressure is less severe.

Simulation Modeling to Assure Relevance

At the end of stage 1 there was agreement on the content of the BSC. Equally important, there was also agreement on the approach forward.

Table 5.1 Intermediate Balanced Score Card (BSC) as developed during the first stage of modeling

	Objectives	Measures
Financial perspective	Be able to meet continued demand growth	Output per employee
		Percentage outsourcing of
	Keep cost levels in line with agreements	cases
Customer perspective	Deliver a good service for a reasonable price	Customer satisfaction
		Throughput time per case
Process perspective	Improve company agility	Throughput time per case
	Reduce work pressure and employee stress in general	% of small and easy cases
		Number of *successful* projects
		Working at home
Learning and growth perspective	Attract and retain good people	Employee turnover rates
	Increase collaboration between employees	Employee satisfaction
		Training on the job/coaching
		Hiring of new staff through referral by colleagues

Especially relevant was that the team felt pleased with their first BSC, but at the same time was very uncertain about its quality. Were these really the right indicators? Had they been complete? And would all the chosen indicators indeed work toward the same goal? What target values for these indicators would be needed to achieve the overall company mission? On the other hand, were some KPIs perhaps redundant? Could the list of KPIs not be shortened further? After all, the fewer dials to watch the easier it becomes to monitor performance effectively. To address these uncertainties, the team decided that a quantified system dynamics simulation model had to be developed.

In the second stage of the project we developed a quantified simulation model for FLA. We started from the causal loop diagrams and the intermediate BSC that had been developed in the first stage. These were sufficient to develop the first skeleton of a system dynamics (SD) model. This skeleton was then filled with key company data, which were delivered by two managers from the MT. These two were more closely involved than the others in the subsequent development of the model, critiquing intermediate versions and providing valuable feedback, fulfilling what Richardson and Andersen (1997) have called a "gatekeeper role".

Accept Worse-Before-Better Performance

With the calibrated simulation model that was developed in this manner, the modelers conducted a number of analyses that addressed the questions the MT was still grappling with after the first stage. This process led to significant additional managerial insights. Firstly, it was comforting for the team to see that most of the KPIs selected for the intermediate version of the BSC were confirmed by the simulation exercises as key in driving performance in the simulation model.

Secondly, what was less comforting for management to notice was the model's suggestion that performance would first deteriorate further before things would get better. The increase in workload that had been building up the past two years would stabilize in the year ahead before it would drop significantly. As a result, setting ambitious targets for especially the first half of the coming year was not appropriate. This was a message that none of the action-oriented managers really liked, but one that was key in managing expectations adequately. This was extremely hard to swallow for the managers. Fortunately, the Director took the lead in embracing this counterintuitive finding.

Outsourcing as a Pressure Valve

Management then moved on quickly to implement a number of mutually reinforcing measures, all aimed at increasing productivity, rather than simply increasing the workforce.

As a quick fix to reduce workloads, legal cases were outsourced to external specialists. At first, the costs of doing so appeared too high. However, a different contractual setup was chosen with a few of the law firms. They would get a guaranteed minimum number of cases per year, both simple and complex ones, but all based on a fixed fee. As a result, rates per cases dropped some 60–70%.

Changing Workflows and Mindsets

With outsourcing as a temporary measure to let off steam, management moved on to make some more structural changes to the organization:

- Organization became based on type of law while it had been regional. This increased productivity, as lawyers were doing more cases in an area they were already proficient in.

- A more efficient method of hiring was developed. Hiring moved from continuous to in three batches per year. As a result, classes could be set up for new hires. These new hires could be trained with far fewer experienced staff than before. This freed up scarce resources.
- A new computerized case allocation system was put in place. This matched new incoming cases with available capacity. The system would also look at the type of skill that would be required for this particular skill. It would try to match this to the skill sets of specific employees.

Hiring with Moderation

All these productivity-boosting measures reduced the need to hire huge numbers of staff. Indeed, it is evident from the numbers that this business unit managed to increase productivity, as measured in Cases handled per Full-Time Equivalent (FTE) with 33% in just 4 years. This is shown in Table 5.2:

This is remarkable, since a Pavlovian reaction for management remains to "throw people at a problem". In the words of the Director: "The first reaction was: we need more people. (…) but solutions sometimes lay on the ground where nobody sees them." The simulation analysis confirms that this was a particularly wise policy, since aggressive hiring would have led to a substantial overshoot, as Fig. 5.3 clearly shows. With a hiring rate where management tries to solve the workload issues within 1 year (line 1), staff more than doubles. This also doubles the costs. More moderate levels of hiring were much more in line with historical reality.

Table 5.2 Cases, FTE and productivity from 2000 to 2004

Year	FTE	Cases	Cases per FTE
2000	237	43.000	181
2001	250	47.000	188
2002	271	54.900	203
2003	303	68.000	224
2004	316	76.300	241

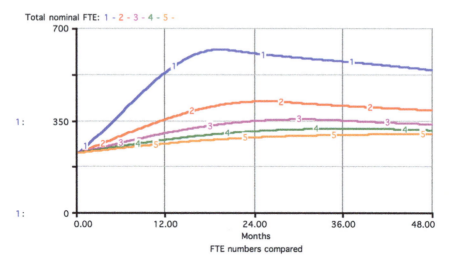

Fig. 5.3 Workforce numbers for hiring delays of 1–5 years

5.4   CONCLUSION

In services in general, and in professional services in particular, a firm's key assets walk out of the door every evening: the employees. When conditions change, the changes in the workforce will decide if the change is a success or a failure. Managing staff well means keeping a whole range of feedback loops simultaneously under control. More work and so more workload leads to stress, which leads to errors, and it leads to burnout and dissatisfied staff. Burnout and errors lead to lower productivity, which further increases workloads. Dissatisfied staff will lead to unhappy customers since staff behavior will not be optimal. Dissatisfied staff also tend to leave, which leads to greater capacity issues, work pressures, and so on.

When staff work hard they also learn more, which raises their productivity, but usually this is a long-term effect that does not help to get through a growth crisis. Demand management can be a short-term fix in such ties: saying no to customers or outsourcing work. The best policy remains to combine working hard on increasing productivity with perseverance during the hard time and moderate hiring. Hiring and subsequent training should take place at an accelerated pace, but without sacrificing quality. Here too, thoughtfulness should be combined with haste. Or, as the motto is of this book: *festina lente.*

REFERENCES

Akkermans, H. A., & van Oorschot, K. E. (2005). Relevance assumed: A case study of balanced scorecard development using system dynamics. *Journal of the Operational Research Society, 56,* 931–941.

Cyert, R., & March, J. (1963). *A behavioral theory of the firm.* Englewood Cliffs: Prentice-Hall.

Miller, G. (1956). The magical number seven, plus or minus two: Some limits on our capacity for processing information. *Psychological Review, 63,* 81–96.

Richardson, G. P., & Andersen, D. F. (1997). Scripts for group model building. *System Dynamics Review, 13*(2), 107–120.

Simon, H. (1957). *Administrative behavior: A study of decision-making processes in administrative organizations.* New York: Macmillan.

Vennix, J. A. M. (1996). *Group model building: Facilitating team learning using system dynamics.* Chichester: Wiley.

CHAPTER 6

Interacting with the Innovators:
Innovation Tipping Points

Abstract There can be such a thing as too much innovation. Increasingly, services live in a digital and disruptive world, and as a result need innovations, usually digital ones, at a very high pace. But this pace can also be set too high. This is what happened at a European telecom company. It then started having increasing performance problems in its digital TV (DTV) services as a result of its relentless pursuit of innovation. Every innovation comes with its set of initially undiscovered bugs and flaws. When these become active, they drain scarce capacity aimed at Quality Assurance (QA) and fixing of bugs away for incident solving. So when innovation rates become too high, they may pass a tipping point and service performance can collapse completely.

There can also be such a thing as too much innovation. Increasingly, services live in a digital and disruptive world, and as a result need innovations, usually digital ones, at a very high pace. But this pace can also be set too high. This is what happened at a European telecom company that had gone through its early ramp-up years with flying colors. It then started having increasing performance problems precisely as a result of its relentless pursuit of innovation.

6.1   FROM PROBLEM CHILD TO PRODIGY

One reason why service supply chains often face problems is that they need to combine a high degree of innovativeness with high reliability of the service. Digital TV (DTV) is such a type of service. DTV is TV offered by telecom operators that runs over broadband Internet. It provides customers with a high level of interactivity with television, so that customers can order, rent, record, or replay their preferred or missed programs, and also watch them online via laptops, tablets, and smart phones.

Such an Over-The-Top (OTT) service is in a race with a broad array of competitors aiming to win customer preference: cable companies, content providers, YouTube, Apple TV, pirate websites offering live transmissions, Pay-tv channels, and so on. Here, *high innovativeness* is required to offer similar functionality or it can lose appeal with today's fickle customers. *High reliability* is also required because minor blips in the quality of the transmission, which would go unnoticed during an Internet browsing session or even in a telephone conversation, can lead to customer complaints. Of all the services provided through copper wire or fiberglass, DTV is arguably the one with the highest required reliability.

In the case study, DTV had historically been a problem child. The European telecom operator under study had recognized the complexities of this service early on. It had been determined not to let such a vulnerable service go down in a premature ramp-up, and it hadn't. Over the years, this had become a major building block for the customer base. However, in 2011 and 2012 the service was facing more and more problems. The prodigy was in trouble.

A Complex IT-Enabled Service Supply Chain

One of the obvious reasons for performance problems is the complex IT architecture over which this type of service has to be delivered. The more systems, stages, and workflows touch a service, the more chances there are that something goes wrong.

As a typical telco network, the Internet access network does not only serve DTV broadcasting, but it also carries out voice and Internet transmission. This implies that multiple Innovation and Operations departments have access to the same physical network, and any change made by innovation or maintenance in any part of the network has potential influence on the end-to-end performance of DTV service.

High Performance Demanded

Another reason for the performance problems is that performance has to be much higher for DTV than for many other services. People will accept while browsing that their Internet connection is down a few seconds. They will not accept the same quality of service when watching an important program on TV.

Steady Growth, Huge Installed Base

Neither at this time, nor in its past, did DTV have major issues with handling new customers. The company had managed to keep growth at a steady and modest pace. After a service has been in existence for some time, problems with the installed base become more important than problems with new customers. During the first years a service exists, the number of customers that joins per month can be 2–10% of the total installed base. If those new customers then call 10–20 times more often than the installed base customers, they can account for a disproportionate amount of service operations attention. However, once a service has more than, say, a few hundred thousand customers, such ramp-up problems become relatively less important.

This is a basic example of stocks-and-flows logic as visualized in Fig. 6.1. As time goes by, the magnitude of the problems caused by the installed base becomes bigger while the size of the customer growth rate increases, but at a much lower rate. This often means a reorientation of management and staff toward better management of the installed base. At this time, the installed base was already over a million users, which is a huge number of customers to monitor.

Fig. 6.1 The stock and flow logic of customer growth versus issue origins

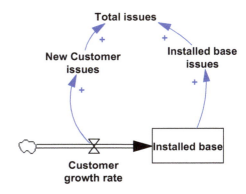

Intermittent Service Breakdowns

There were more and more issues with the installed base. Major service breakdowns, affecting significant parts of the customer base, would occur out of the blue, most of them just in time from creating a massive performance impact. Internally, the company had a system of coding incidents in different colors depending on their customer impact. Blue was a modest impact, yellow was significant, orange was big, red was massive.

Figure 6.2 shows how many incidents of what type occurred in the 2010–2012 period. The 2010 period incident was more of the teething problems kind. They were also all blue, so minor in customer impact. From 2011, the problems changed in nature. Now, their origins were less clear. A code red incident occurred early in 2012, but already in the year before there were quite a few "near misses". For example:

- *May 2011*: Just before 6 p.m. (prime time) key stations were brought back online, fortunately two of a company total of three experts were physically present. In the end, a broken mouse caused the incident. This malfunction suggested that the entire system was down, but only the mouse was.
- *June 2011*: Major impact 50,000+subscribers. Fortunately, the incident took place during office hours. Confusion occurred because,

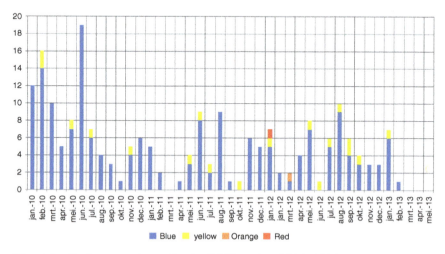

Fig. 6.2 Performance issues for the DTV service, 2010–2012

simultaneously, there were cleanup activities of the CRM (Customer Relationship Management) databases.

- *July 2011*: DTV licenses in one region almost down. Within a few hours all licenses would have been outdated, making service unavailable. The technical expert that provided the solution happened to be shopping with his wife in town on that Saturday. By coincidence, he had heard of some planned maintenance work in the region. The technician who had done this was not aware of any error made.

- *Aug 2011*: Video on Demand servers almost completely filled up before problem was resolved. Hardly any customer impact; else entire customer base would not be able to stream videos.

From these examples it was clear that major service interruptions, hurting a large part of the installed base, were just around the corner. So far, the organization had been "lucky". Structurally speaking, it was too vulnerable to disruptions. Indeed, the first "red" incident occurred in early 2012, although this had its origins from outside of the domain of DTV.

Time Pressure and Shortage of Expert Staff

Time pressure was a huge issue for the DTV operation team during the incident fixing process. The service impacted needed to be restored as soon as possible, especially when the incident happened to a large customer base. Sometimes the service restoration had to be done with a small patch of customers as a trial before it could be further implemented with a bigger patch. With a large customer base impacted, the operational team needed to perform several repetitive fixings in different customers patched in order to fully restore the service.

Given the complexity in the delivery network, experts with end-to-end knowledge of the DTV service and its infrastructure were highly needed. However, they were a scarce resource. There remained only a few people at the DTV operation team who had knowledge about the entire network. So, diagnostic skills were in short supply. And in periods where incidents occurred frequently, the DTV operation team often faced a shortage of available operational resources to carry out the required subsequent fixing activities.

6.2   ROOT CAUSES: TOO MUCH OF A GOOD THING

The problems with this very successful service were partly rooted in the same reasons why it was so successful, in particular its high pace of innovation.

Relentless Innovation

In 2011–2012 there were 11 major incidents, so-called Code Yellow incidents. These are summarized in Table 6.1. The first thing that is worth noting is that these all refer to *digital* services.

Next, of those 11, 6 have their origins in *innovations*, in new functionality becoming available. Given the rate of innovation at DTV and the tightly coupled telecom infrastructure that the DTV service required, this is not surprising.

The rate of innovation was relentless. Figure 6.3 shows in 2012 that the range of changes per month was anywhere between 20 and 60. What this figure also suggests is that there is correlation between the rate of changes and the number of service breakdowns. Correlation is not the same as causation, though.

An Outsourced Innovation Service Ecosystem

The rate of innovation in services keeps increasing, with updates in weeks and months, no longer in quarters and years. At the same time, more and

Table 6.1   Root causes for major incidents per type for DTV, 2011–2012

Date	Root cause	Innovation	Maintenance	Human error
May 2011	Reset database			X
Jun 2011	Set-top box software setup	X		
Jul 2011	Server problem			X
Mar 2012	Set-top box software bug	X		
May 2012	Maintenance upgrade out of service window		X	
Jul 2012	Unauthorized untested changes from supplier	X		
Sept 2012	Set-top box firmware bug	X		
Sept 2012	Driver software bug	X		
Oct 2012	Set-top box firmware bug	X		
Oct '26, '12	Wrong list of customers deleted			X
Nov 3, '12	Customer database bug	X		

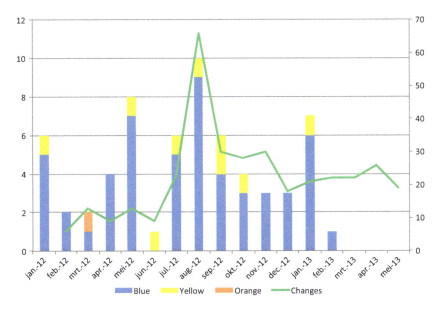

Fig. 6.3 Correlation of innovation output and service breakdowns

more of those innovations are being outsourced. The reasons for this are quality and costs. The skill levels needed to generate this rate of innovation are better available externally. The cost levels of those innovations are lower externally as well. So, there is more innovation and more of it is outsourced to third parties. That doesn't make the coordination with the rest of the service supply chain easier.

What Table 6.1 illustrates is for DTV, and many if not most of these innovations came from outside the company. Much, if not most of the innovation, was outsourced. Set-top boxes caused most of the service disruptions in 2012. These were bought, not made internally. Set-top box firmware was not specified by the company but by the set-top box supplier. The company did have some influence on the software for the set-top box. Another disruption came from a software bug in the customer database, again a product from an outside supplier. All these outside suppliers and service providers collectively formed an innovation service supply chain for DTV. Actually, the term *service network* (Koza and Lewin 1999) or even *service ecosystem* (Vargo and Akaka 2012) would probably describe this situation better.

Fundamentally, any change introduced by the innovations function had potential direct or indirect impact on service performance received by customers. The operations teams were firefighting these incidents under considerable pressure. Meanwhile, driven by the pressures from the market, the innovation teams kept up the pace of the development, quite unaware of the resulting performance impact on service performance.

Bespoke Services, Generic Infrastructure

The same notion of a service supply network or even service ecosystem can be applied to the delivery of the DTV service itself. The DTV service was a bespoke service, but it was delivered over a generic infrastructure. And so, the overall network performance was an important driver for many of the problems with the delivery of the DTV service. This made diagnosis of malfunctions even more difficult. Who had sufficient expertise of not only the DTV-specific infrastructure, but also the overall generic infrastructure?

Undiscovered Innovation Rework

If most of the service interruptions come from innovations, a first option might be to reduce the *quantity* of innovations. However, given the context of this case, it will be clear that this is not really an option in this business. A second option would be to improve the *quality* of these innovations, higher quality in terms of a lower *number of bugs* in the software changes being introduced. It is a fact of life that every innovation carries with it a certain number of undiscovered flaws, or bugs. We also mentioned this in the discussion on the Rework Cycle in Sect. 3.2. A central role in this rework cycle is played by the stock of undiscovered rework, or, in this case, undiscovered bugs (Abdel-Hamid and Madnick 1991). The root cause for incidents lies with until-then undiscovered bugs. These bugs are located in past software changes in the ITV systems infrastructure, both ITV specific and general, where they remain dormant until they become activated by some combination of factors. It is these bugs that generate the performance incidents. Any policy that fails to keep the number of undiscovered bugs under control is bound to fail in the long run.

Figure 6.4 shows a key set of flows that describe the basic structure of the relations between innovation work, bugs, and incident occurrences. It is based on group model-building workshops (Vennix 1996) with key staff from the DTV service supply chain, including innovation, operations, and

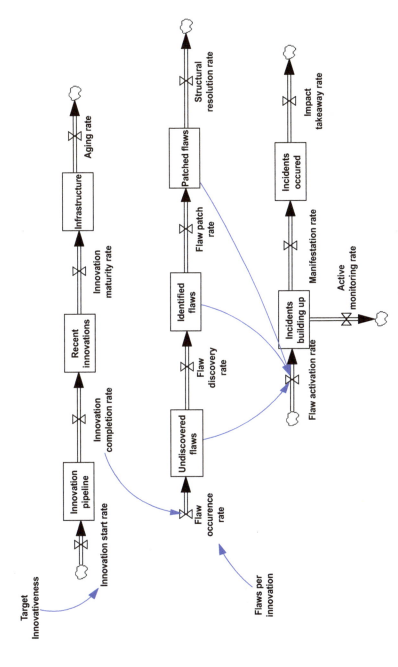

Fig. 6.4 Interrelated flows of innovations, bugs, and incidents for DTV

incident management. It is also based on existing system dynamics models of software projects (Abdel-Hamid and Madnick 1991) and project management (Lyneis and Ford 2007). It shows that with every completed innovation, a certain number of undiscovered flaws are being introduced. These flaws can be identified through Quality Assurance (QA) work before they become active, and then they become identified flaws. When they are fixed they are called "patches". Patching is not quite the same as structurally fixed flaws but at least they have a lower likelihood of leading to flaws.

When flaws are activated, usually by some combination of events, they become incidents in the making: a server database starts to fill up, a software license is not renewed, a connection is down, synchronization no longer works. Once such incidents in the making pass a certain threshold they manifest themselves. Sometimes that can take a long time. When a few dozen customers are affected by the incident every week, probably this will remain unnoticed for a long time amid the hundreds of small and diverse incidents that occur with an installed base of over a million users. Normally, these incidents do not go away automatically. Their impact has to be taken away by human intervention. In summary, the more the innovation, the more the undiscovered flaws, the more the incidents building up, and the more the service interruptions.

Tipping Point Behavior

A quantified version of the model shown in Fig. 6.4 leads to a deeper understanding of what happens to service reliability when a tipping point in innovation is passed.

What happens if after 50 weeks the *desired innovativeness* of the service is increased? Rather than 40% of the functionality being less than 1 year old, the new policy becomes that 50% of all functionality should be new. This is shown in Fig. 6.5. The market appreciates these innovations, and the "Mark" the company gets on innovativeness from the customer gradually grows from "7" to "just under 8" on a 10-point scale. So, the policy appears to be achieving what it intended.

However, every new innovation has its own "teething problems". Every new innovation introduces new bugs, which initially remain undiscovered, as Fig. 6.6 shows.

This increased *bug occurrence rate* leads to a gradual accumulation of undiscovered bugs. Many of these are discovered by QA work, but not all. Fortunately, more and more of these bugs become patched first and finally structurally resolved.

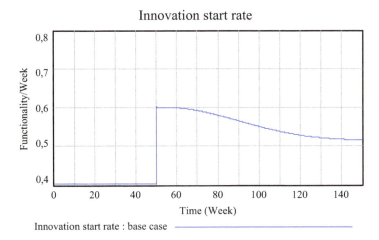

Fig. 6.5 Direct effect of a sudden increase in desired innovativeness

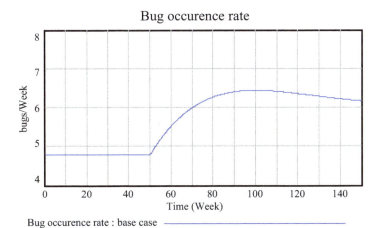

Fig. 6.6 Unintended side effects: bug occurrences after a sudden increase in innovation rate

Where does the increase of bugs lead to? Well, not all bugs immediately manifest themselves and lead to performance issues; many remain hidden or too small to observe. But a certain percentage of them do lead to performance problems, and a fixed percentage of an ever-growing pile of bugs leads to an ever-growing inflow of performance problems. This becomes clear in Fig. 6.7. As there is a steadily increasing pile of bugs, there is a correspondingly steadily growing *manifestation rate of bugs* that actually start affecting performance.

When a bug becomes active it doesn't mean that customers are immediately affected, certainly not in huge numbers. Therefore, it is possible to monitor performance continuously and spot performance issues early on, while they are still under the radar screen of the call center help desk, for instance. This we call *active monitoring* (a non-telecom term with wider usage would be condition-based maintenance [or "CBM"], Jardine et al. 2006). In Fig. 6.8 one can see how this active monitoring rate starts to peak as active bugs become very prominent, from week 90 or so onward. Strangely enough, this active monitoring rate *drops off strongly* after week 120, although the number of active bugs keeps increasing steadily.

As a result, the number of bugs that manifest themselves in performance to the customer base keeps increasing steadily from week 120 onward, where it has been kept in containment to some extent up to that time. Accordingly, the *impact takeaway rate* increases exponentially as well around that time, as shown in Fig. 6.9. With impact takeaway rate we mean that the immediate impact is indeed removed but that a structural solution has not yet been found.

What impact do these performance issues have on market perception? This is shown in Fig. 6.10. Here, the unintended side effect from a laudable effort to improve innovativeness of the service becomes visible. The market appreciates the increased innovativeness of the service. However, *service reliability* goes down the drain completely in the 2 years after the start of the innovation-driven regime.

As a result, customer appreciation of service reliability drops from a cool "7" and even almost an "8" to a miserable "2" in Year 3. The net result of this is, when we give both effects equal weight, shown in Fig. 6.11, *market reputation* completely collapses in Year 3 from "7.3" to "3". The innovation policy has failed utterly, because of the unintended side effects of the intended focus on more innovations.

This is an example of the emergence of structural erosion of quality as an unintended side effect of biased managerial policies. Other examples are of firefighting in product development (Repenning et al. 2001) and of quality erosion in the insurance sector (Oliva and Sterman 2001).

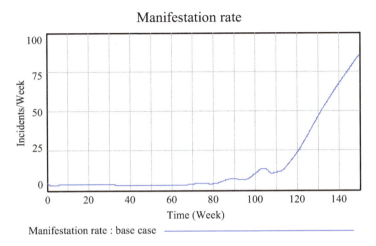

Fig. 6.7 Bugs manifesting as incidents after innovation increase

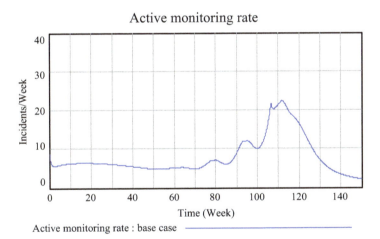

Fig. 6.8 Active monitoring of small incidents after a sudden increase in the innovation rate

A Capability Trap Sucking Staff Toward Firefighting

How is this downward spiral of performance generated? Another part of the model shows the answer, which can be seen as a special case of the so-called *capability trap* that haunts many organizations under pressure (Repenning

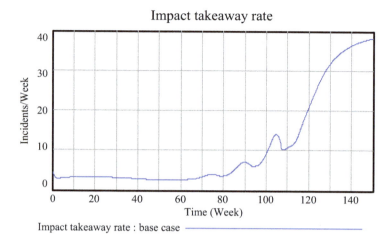

Fig. 6.9   Growth of impact takeaway rate after innovation increase

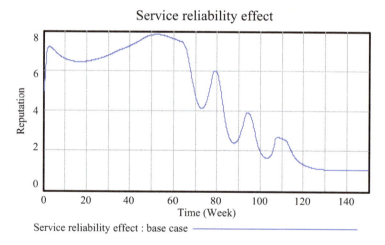

Fig. 6.10   Effect of sudden increase in innovation rate on subsequent service reliability

and Sterman 2002). A common analogy is that of the lumberjack who is seen working as hard as he can, chopping wood with a blunt axe. When asked why he doesn't sharpen the axe he replies that he doesn't have the time, as he has too much wood chopping left to do. Something similar happens also in this system, as the graphs in Fig. 6.12 illustrate.

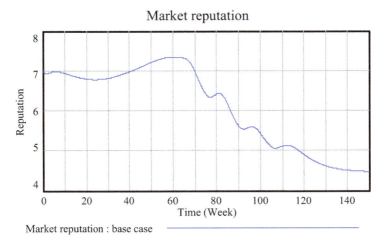

Fig. 6.11 Combined effect of service reliability and perceived innovativeness on market reputation

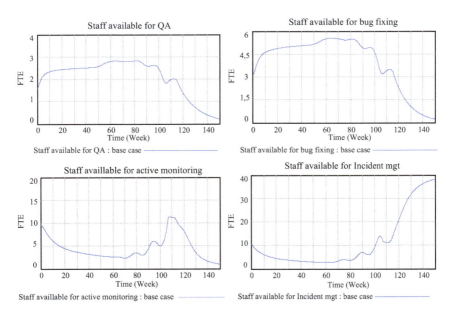

Fig. 6.12 Allocation of staff between bug fixing and incident management

In this model there are three capacity groups: people focused on *innovation*, staff working on *QA & bug fixing*, and operational people dealing with *incident management* and resolution. The staff involved in innovation remains stationary in the base case. But the allocation of staff dealing with bug fixing is very dynamic. Initially, the bulk of the staff lined up for bug fixing is mostly concentrated around structural solutions for bugs. Gradually, the two other types of staff gain more clout, both at the expense of the structural solutions activity and at the expense of the staff working on incident management.

This changes over the course of Year 2, when the increase in innovations leads to more and more bugs. Then, the *staff available for QA* as well as *staff for bug fixing* increases, and structural fix activity drops off.

Toward the end of Year 2, from Week 80 onward, all types of bug fixing work suffer, as more and more people are drawn toward incident management. First, most of the action in incident management is still on the preventive side, in *active monitoring*, with an absolute peak around Week 110. But after that, it is no longer possible to even focus on active monitoring, and all staff is drawn toward the ultimate form of firefighting, which is *incident management* (the bottom right graph in Fig. 6.12).

All this behavior is generated endogenously, through proportional allocation of capacity (Sterman 2000). Please note that the amount of work involved in incident management is far greater than the amount of work required to timely eradicate the bug that eventually leads to this incident.

6.3   SYSTEMIC SOLUTIONS

This case is one example where *festina lente* is not the first systemic policy that comes to mind. The competition for DTV is relentless, and so the rate of innovation has to be kept high or the entire service will gradually become obsolete. Going slow to go fast is not an obvious choice here. Being thoughtful and systemic about what to do best remains good advice. Let's return to what lies at the core of the rising number of incidents: undiscovered rework.

Keep Undiscovered Rework Low

The stable situation in our simulation exercise collapses because the inflow of undiscovered rework becomes structurally greater than the outflow, the

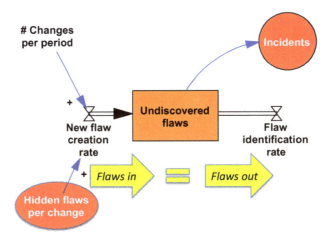

Fig. 6.13 The root problem of high innovation rates: undiscovered flaws

flaw identification rate. This is visualized in Fig. 6.13. Problem containment is not possible in the base case: there is not enough capacity to keep the rate of flaws-out equal to the rate of flaws-in. So, what can be done?

If we focus on the inflow first: as indicated, we assume that reducing the rate of innovation, and thus the number of changes in functionality per period, is not an option. What is an option is the number of hidden flaws per innovation. In the logic of *Poka Yoke*, this would be a key guiding principle. Unfortunately, every sector has its share of undiscovered bugs. However, if the rate of innovation increases with 50% and we reduce the number of bugs with 33%, then the net inflow of bugs would remain stable.

Proportional Increase of Staff

The next best thing would be to have great QA. That means more staff there, that is, enough staff to keep the discovery rate of bugs at least equal to the new bug creation rate. The next step down the chain then would be various forms of bug fixing capacity. However, the capacity needed to fix one bug is greater than the capacity needed to spot a bog. And the capacity needed to solve one incident is considerably more than the time needed to fix a bug.

There is no such thing as a free lunch. If management wants to increase output of one stage of this capacitated service supply chain with 50%, it will have to increase the capacities for the other stages as well. And as these subsequent steps require more man-hours per bug/incident tackled, the staff increase will have to be proportionally greater as well.

Throbbing Between Two Lives: *Pooling of Operations and Innovation*

Management of DTV actually tried one policy that was successful at the time. This was to have staff from Innovation chip in with Operations during a period in which there were just too many incidents. Indeed, Fig. 6.14 shows that when innovation staff helped to fix bugs in completed functionality, a performance collapse could be prevented. This figure shows historical case data for the call ratio at the customer care center for DTV, as a proxy for incidents occurrence. It also shows the number of changes in functionality introduced per week. Both indicators exhibit considerable variation over time.

The period of interest is the fourth quarter of 2012. There is both a record number of changes and, shortly afterward, a peak in the call ratio. In response, management decided to relocate staff to Operations to fix bugs, and help in root cause analysis and incident management. In the next quarter, the call ratio went down considerably. So, this policy worked, apparently. It also made good sense, as the innovation staff often has in-depth knowledge of the systems that are generating the bugs. On the other hand, the rate of new changes also dropped, which is only logical, since innovation staff is not busy implementing additional innovations.

Moreover, in the longer run such pooling will lead to oscillations, or as the poet T.S. Elliot phrased it, as "throbbing between two lives". The key reason for these oscillations is the delays that are involved in transferring staff from one group to the next. Before the switch, staff members need to finish what they were working on, they may have to move to another building, they need to figure out how to help their colleagues in the other group, and so on. So, there is a setup time involved. By the time the staff members are fully productive in their new group, another group may be starved for resources, and a new transfer may be required.

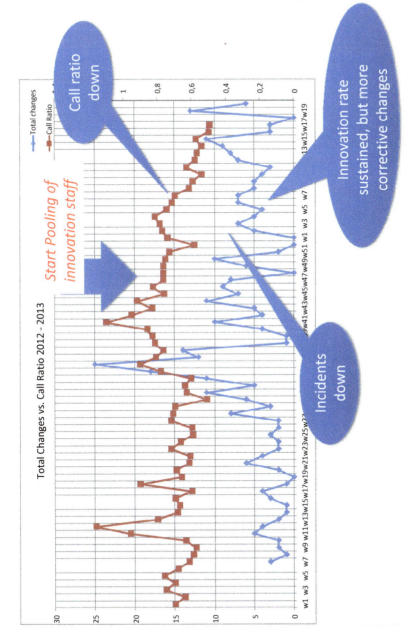

Fig. 6.14 Functionality change rates and call ratios in 2012–2013

Condition Monitoring

Customers first noted almost all the service breakdowns and started to call the customer care center. When it became obvious there that the number of customers calling with the same problem was unusually high, they would consult Operations. Almost none of the significant service breakdowns were first observed by Operations and resolved before customers started calling in numbers.

In fact, analysis of the major breakdowns in 2011–2012 suggests that most of these breakdowns could have been foreseen on the basis of data that was available internally beforehand. However, this data was not used for this purpose. In theory, one should be able to observe and resolve all incidents before customers do. In other sectors, such as the process industry or aerospace, such CBM practices are much more widespread (Jardine et al. 2006). In 2012–2013, the general mindset was one of corrective maintenance, which is by definition maintenance that is done too late.

Even corrective maintenance can be done more and less effectively. Very complex systems can have so many failure modes that it becomes impractical to monitor all the data that will provide early warning indicators for functionality that is about to break. In such settings, corrective maintenance is the best one can do. However, corrective maintenance can be done both really fast or not fast at all. Fast is usually effective, not fast isn't.

Figure 6.15 shows that corrective maintenance for the major incidents in 2011–2012 was not fast at all. The biggest delay in solving was consistency in incident discovery. What if through better monitoring, this incident discovery period could be reduced to just a few minutes? This is possible but requires a systematic approach toward all the key failure modes for a rigorous FMECA (Failure Mode, Effect, and Criticality Analysis). Given the time pressures involved, and the scarcity of true experts of the entire DTV infrastructure, who would be available to conduct such FMECAs?

6.4   Conclusion

In digital and disruptive services, the interactions of innovation staff with operations are numerous and tight. The rate of innovations is such that without knowledge of what has been recently added in new functionality, dealing with operational issues becomes impossible.

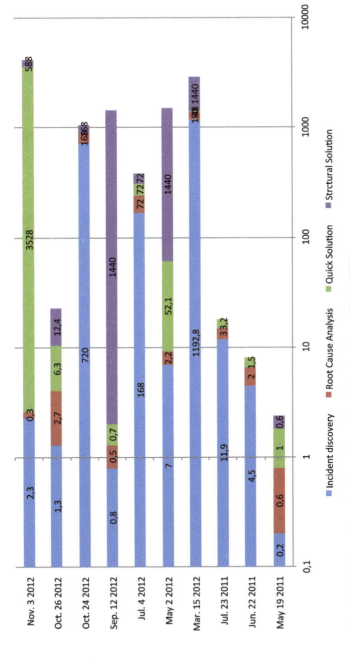

Fig. 6.15 Time delays in discovering and solving incidents, 2011–2012

It is tempting for management to target for increased innovation rates, as this is the way to win against the competition in these innovation-driven markets. However, asking more output from a supply chain does not come without making extra investments as well. At the very least, more staff will be needed to deal with the extra work that more innovations will generate. Innovations generate extra work because they always come with undiscovered bugs. Over time, these bugs will turn into performance incidents if they are not discovered and fixed timely.

Innovation-driven supply chains can easily pass a tipping point of innovativeness and collapse in a mess of performance issues. A tempting strategy that works in the short and medium term is to pool Innovation and Operations staff together, and have the designers of the recent innovations fix the bugs they unintentionally created. However, in the longer run this leads to undesirable oscillations of workloads and innovation rates. Having fewer bugs per innovation is the *Poka Yoke* approach that would be best. Moving to a system with a much more sophisticated active monitoring that would signal performance issues quickly before they grow big would be the next best thing. However, both policies require a major and sustained effort to improve quality. It will require a truly wise and determined management team to implement such strategies. Indeed, the Ancients would appreciate such sustained determination.

REFERENCES

Abdel-Hamid, T., & Madnick, S. (1991). *Software project dynamics: An integrated approach.* Englewood Cliffs: Prentice-Hall.
Jardine, A. K., Lin, D., & Banjevic, D. (2006). A review on machinery diagnostics and prognostics implementing condition-based maintenance. *Mechanical Systems and Signal Processing, 20*(7), 1483–1510.
Koza, M. P., & Lewin, A. Y. (1999). The coevolution of network alliances: A longitudinal analysis of an international professional service network. *Organization Science, 10*(5), 638–653.
Lyneis, J. M., & Ford, D. N. (2007). System dynamics applied to project management: A survey, assessment, and directions for future research. *System Dynamics Review, 23,* 157–189.
Oliva, R., & Sterman, J. D. (2001). Cutting corners and working overtime: Quality erosion in the service industry. *Management Science, 47*(7), 894–914.
Repenning, N., & Sterman, J. (2002). Capability traps and self-confirming attribution errors in the dynamics of process improvement. *Administrative Science Quarterly, 47,* 265–295.

Repenning, N. P., Goncalves, P., & Black, L. J. (2001). Past the tipping point: The persistence of firefighting in product development. *California Management Review, 43*(4), 44–63.

Sterman, J. D. (2000). *Business dynamics: Systems thinking and modeling for a complex world.* New York: McGraw-Hill.

Vargo, S. L., & Akaka, M. A. (2012). Value cocreation and service systems (re) formation: A service ecosystems view. *Service Science, 4*(3), 207–217.

Vennix, J. A. M. (1996). *Group model building: Facilitating team learning using system dynamics.* Chichester: Wiley.

CHAPTER 7

Interacting with Key Suppliers:
Relationship Spirals

Abstract A special category of stakeholders is that of the key suppliers, or co-makers. The bulk of the service transactions in this world is B2B (Business-to-Business). Moreover, every B2C (Business-to-Consumer) company provides services in co-production with a range of suppliers. In services, often, the consumers will be directly affected by the performance of these suppliers, very different from manufacturing. In service supply chains, the supplier, the service provider, and the customer effectively form a *service triad*. This chapter looks at this phenomenon through the case of a European port authority and its IT outsourcing partner. A winner's curse outsourcing contract and serious maritime incidents led to a vicious relationship spiral. Through a collaborative service design process, parties tried to reverse this spiral into a virtuous one.

A special category of stakeholders is formed by key suppliers, or even co-makers, as they are often called in manufacturing contexts. So far, we have zoomed in on how to deal with customers where the customers were consumers, not businesses. These B2C (Business-to-Consumer) markets characterize the service operations we zoom into in this book. However, the bulk of the business transactions in this world is B2B (Business-to-Business). Moreover, every B2C company provides services in co-production with a whole range of suppliers. Given the special nature of services, often the consumers will be affected by the performance of these suppliers. This is different from manufacturing supply chains, where a component supplier will rarely have direct interaction with an end customer. In service supply chains, the supplier, the service provider, and the customer effectively form a *service triad*, and not a dyad (Choi and Wu 2009; Wynstra et al. 2015).

7.1   AN OUTSOURCING DEAL TURNED SOUR

The case in this chapter concerns an IT outsourcing arrangement between a major European Port Authority and a medium-sized European IT services provider. The Port Authority (hereafter called the Authority) was an autonomous company with two public sector shareholders. Although publicly owned, it was in practice mostly run as a commercial company. The Authority is an entrepreneurial port developer with a stake in various ports around the globe. Part of its strategy is to have its home base offer an ideal showcase to attract customers worldwide with its exemplary performance in efficiency, safety, and sustainability. The IT service provider (ITCo) is a medium-sized IT solution provider for the corporate world. The Authority is not one of its larger customers, but one with high market visibility, nevertheless.

In 2006, the Authority went to the market in order to outsource its generic IT services and IT infrastructure. ITCo won the deal and in the summer of 2007 the IT outsourcing took effect. For a period of 5 years, ITCo would take on the responsibility for the (quality of) IT, whilst having the Authority enjoying ITCo's economies of scale, innovation, and knowledge of market developments. Cost management was an explicit objective. The most important functional areas under the ITO (IT Outsourcing) agreement were the development and subsequent hosting and management of office automation, hosting, and the management of both enterprise resource planning (ERP) and Maritime Applications. ITCo would also render Customer Service toward Authority personnel and that of third parties.

Not Such a Wonderful Deal After All

After this outsourcing deal, both the Authority and the IT vendor reported back home that they had secured a wonderful deal for them. Only it wasn't so for either of them, as would become clear. Not long after the ITO took effect, the Authority felt that notably the IT service with respect to Maritime Applications fell short of expectations. There were multiple incidents in this area, Customer Service was considered poor, and problem resolution time was considered excessive. Notably, the Authority's Division Harbor Master (managing all inbound and outbound traffic in the Port) suffered major disruptions toward its customers. Many so-called escalations toward senior ITCo Management took place, but were apparently not very successful since dissatisfaction of the Authority steadily grew over time.

Vicious Cycle of Low Trust and Performance on Both Sides

Both sides, the IT supplier and the customer, gradually become caught in a vicious cycle of low trust in the other side fed by low performance. This then led to bad communication and bad collaboration on both sides, and this then led to bad performance. This way, the buyer-supplier relation had gone from bad to worse. And performance did not improve, on the contrary.

From One Performance Crisis to Another

When office staff cannot print or cannot have access to certain applications, this is of course very annoying and time-consuming. However, when staff are working in the harbor, making sure that ships unload their cargo safely, such IT problems can have life-threatening effects. And there were more and more of such incidents. When IT is not available for the maritime pilot and deck officers to steer a ship safely into the harbor, the risks of error increase rapidly and the potential consequences of such errors can be extremely high. So there were high potential risks next to the very high number of major incidents that actually occurred.

Figure 7.1 shows in normalized format the major incidents per month and per source. Unfortunately, there are no earlier data available. What this chart does show is that, until mid-2012, the majority of the severe incidents were caused by the supplier. It also shows the success of the turnaround that was realized.

Crisis Management and Turnaround

In an IT outsourcing setting such as this one, both parties have a shared destiny, at least for the duration of the contract. So, they simply have to find a way to collaborate better. However, often the way to do so leads to

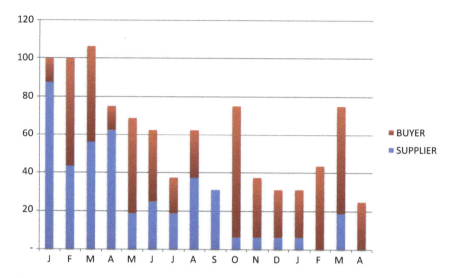

Fig. 7.1   Major incidents per source per month (normalized), 2012–2013

the opposite. Things only get worse, not better. The relationship turned into a crisis.

In 2010 the Authority appointed a new Chief Information Officer (CIO). One of his key tasks was to improve the effectiveness of IT outsourced services. A quick scan convinced him of the ineffectiveness of the IT outsourcing arrangement, as the Service Level Agreements (SLAs) entered into had no direct relation to or impact on the Authority's business parameters: Efficiency, Safety, Security, and Sustainability. He was aware that hassle-free IT was conditional to the Authority achieving its above business objectives. His question, as he put it, was: "How do we install business-linked KPIs into the outsourcing relationship?" Under considerable suspicion on both sides, the author was part of the team that started this change effort.

7.2   Root Causes

The root causes for the service performance problems in this case lie in two main areas. There were a number of primarily *technical*, operational, and relatively objective limitations of the design that was applied, next to a number of mostly *social*, organizational, and inherently subjective processes that took place.

In the first category fall:

- Unfocused service operations design
- Mixed tangibility of performance indicators
- Internal functional silos on both sides
- Problematic attribution of performance results

To the second category belong:

- The winner's curse
- Vicious cycles and relationship spirals
- Micromanagement and organizational inertia
- Incentive misalignments

We will discuss them one by one.

Unfocused Service Operations Design

The concept of the *focused factory* is one of the foundations of operations strategy. Skinner (1974) introduced the concept of the focused factory into the operations management vocabulary. He based his concept on the highly intuitive notion that a plant can achieve superior performance by organizing its resources to perform on one task, instead of trying to meet all sorts of demands from internal and external sources. As a result, a focused factory with a narrow product mix for a particular market niche will outperform the conventional plant, which has a broader scope.

What is true for factories is also true for most service settings (Pieters et al. 2010). In the context of this Harbor Authority case it is a workflow design flaw to have two completely different types of calls dealt with by one and the same customer care unit. The results will be bad for both types of calls, and for the agent involved. And it will be bad, for that matter, for the customer-supplier relationship. Figure 7.2 illustrates the complex workflows that this arrangement could lead to when the agent was unable to resolve the query right away. In the end, this could result in waking up the Harbor Master at night to escalate the issue via the CIO to ITCo's Client Director and all the way back to the operational staff.

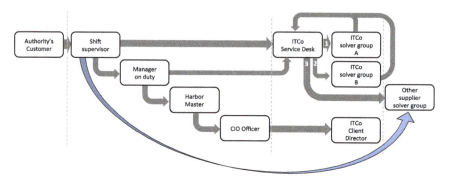

Fig. 7.2 Different possible workflows for a call from the Authority to ITCo

Mixed Tangibility of Performance Indicators

Another classic issue, now from the field of economics, not from operations, is that of mixed tangibility. It has been known for decades that when firms with multiple objectives use strong incentives, those tasks that are easiest to measure tend to attract the most effort, to the detriment of tasks whose output is more difficult to measure (Holmstrom and Milgrom 1991; Roberts 2004). For example, the minutes spent on dealing with a customer call can be easy to determine; the quality of the problem-solving activity of that call is much more difficult to define and measure.

The traditional purchasing approach that emphasizes cost and delivery terms works well enough where specifications are clear and quality is easy to monitor. But in the case of services, where the customer is clearly co-producing with the customer, this is rarely the case. Here, a traditional purchasing approach is likely to fail because the objectives that are easiest to measure will attract the most attention, to the detriment of the other objectives (Parker and Anderson 2002). This clearly was an issue in this case as well.

Internal Functional Silos on Both Sides

In this interorganizational setting, it is obvious to look at the huge walls between customer and supplier. However, there were also multiple walls within the customer and within the supplier. All these walls further complicated the task of aligning across the service supply chain. When he was presented with the actual detailed workflow between ITCo, the Authority's IT department, and his own unit, the Harbor Master commented that he saw a stark difference between what he had "contracted" with his CIO and what IT subsequently had "contracted out" to ITCo.

Problematic Attribution of Performance Results

A core issue in performance-based contracts is how to attribute the results obtained to a specific supplier (and not to other suppliers or to the customer). ITCo wasn't the Authority's only IT supplier. In general, services of suppliers are normally integrated in a greater whole. So, the behavior of other suppliers has an influence on performance, and the behavior of the customer also has an impact, good or bad.

Sampson (2000) has called this the customer-supplier duality: all services have customers as primary suppliers of inputs. After all, as a customer one always has to provide something to the service provider to have the service delivered. That can be:

- information (e.g. what one wants to eat to the restaurant, where one wants to go to the taxi driver)
- assets (e.g. the car to the garage)
- one's body (to the hairdresser, to the physician)

As a result, it becomes problematic to specify an outcome-based contract between buyer and supplier. Also, in the case of the Authority, this made it difficult to specify performance indicators that ITCo had mostly under control.

The Winner's Curse

This outsourcing deal had been a cost-driven one. The detrimental effects of such a cost-driven outsourcing deal become more visible as time goes by. This is the winner's curse at work (Kern et al. 2002). In such a cost-driven outsourcing, both parties may feel that they have won, but over time it becomes apparent that they actually may have lost, not won. The supplier cannot make a profit on the contract, which hurts business. The customer experiences that the supplier cannot invest in improving the service: there is no budget to do so.

Figure 7.3 summarizes the winner's curse that was active during the first phase of the relationship.

In this qualitative case, there are few quantitative data available to back up the argument. Instead, we use extensive quotes from the evaluation interviews with the stakeholders on both sides. These quotes serve to confirm that these causal effects actually played out in the case. We start at the middle left of the loop shown in Fig. 7.3: the customer's focus on short-term cost savings during the outsourcing arrangement in this case. In itself, there is nothing wrong with a cost focus as a key driver for an outsourcing arrangement. Indeed, Lacity et al. (2009) have observed that cost reduction is the most common motive behind IT outsourcing decisions. Nevertheless, cost was a very dominant factor in the decision-making process, as confirmed by both sides. ITCo's VP confirmed that cost focus was predominant in the tender, and the Port Authority also stated that the former CIO had aimed at the cheapest possible deal.

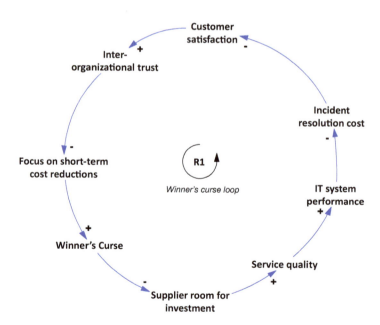

Fig. 7.3 The vicious cycle of the winner's curse in the Port Authority case

In this case, the emphasis on short-term financial gains appears to have been counterproductive in retrospect. On the customer side, the drive to squeeze the supplier to the utmost appears to have been especially strong. On the supplier side, the drive to secure the deal at all costs may have been counterproductive as well. Indeed, one of the ITCo executives in charge confirmed that during the final meeting in which the deal was made, their chief executive took another X% of an already sharp final offer.

So at the time, this may have seemed a well-executed deal on both sides, but in retrospect the Authority may have lost more than it gained, since it had to accept cuts in quality and quantity of IT support in exchange for the lowest price. Because of the limited room for investment with the supplier, service quality suffered over time.

Four years later, in 2011, the need to keep cutting costs that was generated by the original outsourcing contract was still felt. For instance, the customer contact center found its staff dedicated to the Authority's IT business reduced by 25% and merged with other agents so that a pool of staff collectively served several unrelated customers. ITCo's Service Desk manager commented that he feared that with further cost drives he would have to revert to temporary labor or even offshoring, with harmful effects on quality.

Despite this continued efficiency drive, because of the large number of incidents that has to be managed, it remains doubtful if the Authority's business has been all that profitable for ITCo. ITCo higher management believed that they had been losing money on this deal and without much prospect of making significant returns in the future.

We can conclude that there has been a winner's curse in this outsourcing arrangement, and that the limited room for supplier investment has hurt service quality, which are the three first causal steps in Fig. 7.3 moving from the focus on short-term cost reductions. The next causal steps in Fig. 7.3 lead to IT system performance and from thereon to IT incident costs.

These incidents were not only dangerous, but they also led to significant handling costs on both sides. This led to complex, time-consuming, and frustrating workflows when the standard operating procedures did not provide a solution. With such frequent incidents and ineffective lines of communication, customer satisfaction may also suffer seriously from these incidents. In 2009 and 2010, average customer satisfaction for office automation and maritime calls was 6.8 on a 10-point scale at best, and 5.6 at worst, with an average of 6.2 over these 2 years. Two remarks given by anonymous respondents in a client satisfaction survey from May 2009 summarize the general mood:

> *In the past it was much better. The old team had much more experience and knew how to solve the problem quickly. I simply miss the old IT staff!*
>
> *The people who staff the contact centre outside office hours have no idea of what takes place here at the Authority, leave alone of the variety of [maritime] applications and the importance of those.*

One consequence of trust, which is a strong focus on ongoing cost cutting, was implemented into the contract by the customer. The supplier responded by further limiting resources dedicated to this client, driven by the annual reduction on costs in this outsourcing contract. He admitted that in doing so, they hadn't been looking too much at what those would imply for the customer.

A similar unintended side effect of a short-term cost focus could be observed within the Authority itself. There too, budget was too tight to do what was needed to perform well. This cost pressure then further reinforced the winner's curse effect. And so, trust and performance continue to erode.

Vicious Cycles and Relationship Spirals

The problem with erosion of trust and performance is that they can quickly turn into a vicious cycle, or a relationship spiral (Autry and Golicic 2010). In Akkermans et al. (2004) this process was described in the context of supply chain collaboration in the semiconductor industry, but a general formulation of these dynamics is shown in Fig. 7.4.

This causal loop diagram leads as follows. Reinforcing loop R1 shows that when there is high trust, there is little opportunistic behavior, or in plain English cheating, which leads to good decisions. Good decisions lead to good performance, which further builds a history of successful collaboration. This further builds trust. Unfortunately, this loop also works the same way. In a setting of poor performance, trust will erode which will lead to more opportunistic behavior, which will hurt performance even further. Loops R2 and R3, which deal with communication and transparency, reinforce this spiraling effect. This is what is called a relationship spiral, out of which supply chain partners find it very hard to escape.

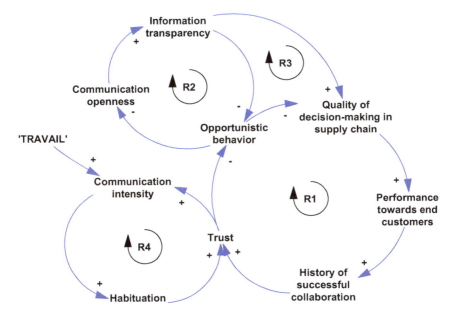

Fig. 7.4 Vicious and virtuous cycles of trust, transparency, and performance. (Adapted from Akkermans et al. 2004)

R4 provides a potential antidote. If supply chain partners work intensively with each other, a process called habituation occurs, which will build trust. Potentially, this can flip a vicious cycle into a virtuous one. We will return to this in the next section.

Micromanagement and Organizational Inertia

This generic process was also found to play out in the Harbor Authority case, but with a particular twist. The continued dissatisfaction with the performance of the supplier, in combination with the continued focus on cost reductions, led the customer to try and manage the activities performed by the IT supplier in high detail. In this case, this led to micromanagement by the customer. That triggered another reinforcing feedback loop, labelled R2, visualized in Fig. 7.5.

We start at the bottom of this causal loop, at the "cost reduction focus" leading to "micromanagement". One example may illustrate this

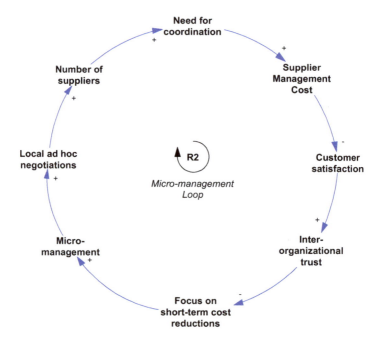

Fig. 7.5 The vicious cycle of micromanagement in the Port Authority case

relationship. In a strive from purchasing to drive acquisition costs down, a Request for Proposals for a certain kind of surveillance camera was split into hardware and software to drive acquisition costs down. However, Total Cost of Ownership went up as result of these two suppliers that had difficulty to align their processes and business requirements. ITCo's initial offering was integrated and would probably have led to lower costs.

Again, both the supplier and the customer suffer from unintended side effects. Often, the requirements from the Division Harbor Master for tailor-made IT applications could only be fulfilled by customized standard solutions. Off-the-shelf solutions were not available for their requirements. This was a problem in the eyes of the Authority Information Management. However, it was also a problem in the eyes of ITCo. They felt that the Port Authority tended to overspecify its outsourcing needs, resulting in very complex sets of requirements.

One other effect of this micromanagement and second-guessing of suppliers such as in the camera acquisition example resulted in a proliferation of suppliers, next to the main outsourcing partner: Such practices proliferated the need for coordination between all these different suppliers and all their respective activities. ITCo's Service Desk did not function as a real single point of contact. Once a call had been put through to one of the other suppliers, ITCo would consider the call closed and the Authority needed to keep chasing the other suppliers themselves.

If there was an issue for which the expertise of another supplier than ITCo was required, both knowledge and coordination issues arose. After all, ITCo had no agreements with our other suppliers, and yet ITCo was the single point of contact for the other suppliers. Little wonder that fulfilling SLAs was often problematic.

This fragmentation of knowledge was true both for the supplier base and for the internal organization. For instance, regarding the network infrastructure, knowledge was scattered around the organization and there was no overall, consolidated knowledge base. Also, a great deal of expertise had been dissipated from the organization following internal mutations. As a result of this, the costs of managing all these supplier-related activities rose considerably. The Authority had many internal business IT demand organizations that would pose requirements toward the CIO Office as the IT supply organization. In its turn, the CIO Office functioned as an IT demand organization toward the Port Authority's suppliers in a management/subcontractor configuration.

All these knowledge sources that needed to give their input and that held parts of the pieces of the puzzle led to slow response times at best. Stakeholders on both sides complained about the large number of links and handovers in the chain that led to time delays and errors transmitted along the way. It was not unusual that the actual execution time to fulfill a request was half an hour, while the process surrounding the request would span 2 or 3 days.

Not surprisingly, this well-intended micromanagement only reinforced the tendency for customer satisfaction to decline. Ironically, the strong focus on cost reduction with the customer that had triggered this chain of events led to higher costs for both the Authority and ITCo in the end. Micromanagement was clearly not the way to effectively align incentives between buyer and supplier in this case.

Incentive Misalignments

We now come to the root of the problem: misalignment of incentives. Again, a number of causal effects collectively generate a vicious cycle. This loop (R3) is visualized in Fig. 7.6.

The focus on short-term cost savings, in combination with low trust levels, engendered misalignment of incentives throughout the process. Not just between buyer and supplier, but also within the Authority and within ITCo. Within ITCo, the situation was not all that different: here too, stovepipes and SLAs flourished.

The rest of this feedback loop is identical to R1. Low focus on quality improvements hurts performance, which further reduces trust. This leads to an even stronger cost drive and we are back at the willingness to partner.

All the feedback loops described so far are reinforcing feedback loops. This means that, without intervention from factors outside of the loop, they will generate behavior that keeps moving in the same direction over time. This can be either a vicious cycle, with ever-lower values, or a virtuous cycle, with ever-higher values. The systemic solutions should therefore be directed toward reversing the vicious cycle into a virtuous one (e.g. Akkermans and van Helden 2002).

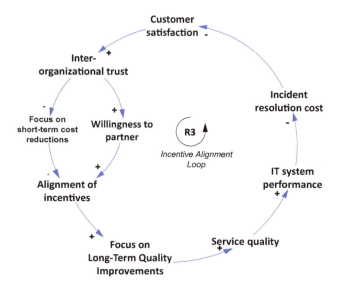

Fig. 7.6 The vicious cycle of incentive misalignment in the Port Authority case

7.3 SYSTEMIC SOLUTIONS

It may now be clear how vicious cycles of low trust, transparency, and organizational traction can generate relationship spirals in IT outsourcing. However, understanding what causes ineffective outsourced service arrangements is different from making them work effectively. In this case, a systemic understanding was generated in a generic three-stage process of analysis, redesign, and implementation of the redesign.

Systemic Root Cause Analysis

To make both organizations aware that something needs no change, and not just the other side, they first have to understand the "the whole elephant", as we have seen in earlier chapters. For this, representatives from all the key stages of the service supply chain spanning both organizations must come together physically. Then they can map out all the key processes and interrelations. This leads to better insight into interconnections between service processes. It also leads to a better understanding of why the other side behaves the way they do. Ultimately, it also leads to a better understanding of the ways in which the own organization is unintentionally generating undesirable behavior on the other side. In this case, representatives from both the Harbor Authority and ITCo came together for 2 days in an off-site location to work on this. Here, the group produced intermediate versions of the process flows and causal loops as shown in the previous section. In the process, they also created transparency and trust on both sides.

End-of-Process KPIs

When it becomes clear how both parties can help and hurt each other, it also becomes clear what good KPIs for both sides are. What KPIs can best be monitored to make sure that a desired state of affairs is achieved? Ideally, the supplier and the customer use the same performance indicators to monitor their performance.

This usually means that these have to be so-called end-of-process KPIs. At the end of the various processes in the service supply chain, the service to the "customer base" of the customer is determined. Performance here determines the success of the customer. The supplier will have an impact on that performance, but not completely. So, the trick is to make smart choices for KPIs here and to create mutual trust.

Service Operations Redesign

Often, a joint mapping exercise reveals illogical workflows and demarcations of responsibilities. From a joint systemic perspective, it becomes obvious that these can and should be redesigned. Figure 7.7 explains how the problems that this service supply chain was facing were not different before, but the approach to tackle them was. Earlier the emphasis had been on functional boundaries and demarcations. The approach had been to monitor lots of detailed SLAs. Now, the group sought to develop a small set of business-driven KPIs together, and install service supply chain-wide coordination mechanisms.

Implementation

In the half year that followed, four work groups with clearly interlinked tasks and goals produced a coherent set of measures, redesigns, and KPIs. The logic linking these subgroups was first developed during the diagnostic phase and further refined in this period. The picture in Fig. 7.8 visually summarizes this logic.

Four work groups had been defined, staffed with representatives from both organizations:

1. Mobilization
2. Knowledge management

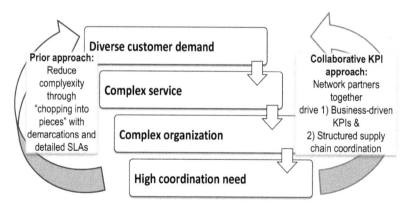

Fig. 7.7 Explanation of change approach in the Port Authority case

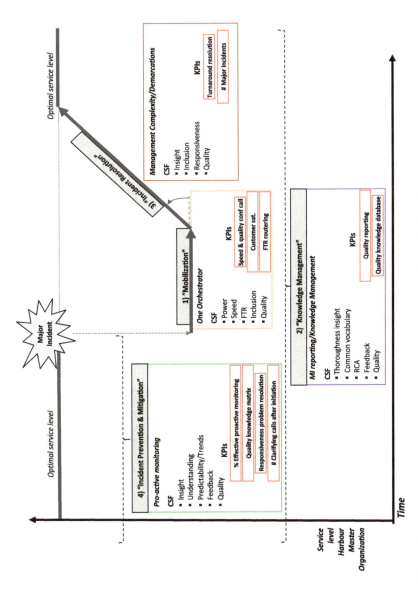

Fig. 7.8 Interlinkages between work groups and KPIs in the Port Authority case

3. Incident resolution
4. Incident prevention and mitigation

As can be seen in this picture, these four topics all have their own role in making sure that the service level of the Harbor Authority toward its customers stays optimal.

- *Incident prevention* had as its goal to make sure that incidents do not happen, or remain small. As is evident from Fig. 7.1, this was done very successfully in this period.
- *Mobilization* takes over when a major incident still occurs. Its main role is to get all parties needed to resolve the incident together as quickly as possible. The KPIs here are aimed at mobilizing the resources needed to resolve the issues.
- *Incident resolution* gets service back to normal as soon as possible. The turnaround time is an obvious key KPI here. Note that this is a performance indicator that both parties influence, not just the IT supplier.
- *Knowledge management* is always in the background, making sure that there is a common vocabulary and sharing of insights, to facilitate the effectiveness of the three other groups.

7.4   Conclusion

Behind every successful B2C service stand a number of strategic B-2-B (Business-to-Business) relations with key suppliers. These key suppliers form a service triad together with the customer base and the focal service firm, who is both a buyer and a supplier of services. Managing relations with such key suppliers, who are effectively co-makers for the focal firm, is very difficult. Working from a performance-based contract is tempting for the focal firm but tricky because, in services, they co-produce the service together with their supplier. In such a setting, to whom should responsibility for results be allocated?

Often, such service settings result in buyer-supplier relationship spirals. Here, trust and transparency on both sides are low because performance is low, which further hurts trust and transparency. The challenge is to reverse such a vicious cycle into a virtuous one. This is possible through a systemic and collaborative change effort. Such change initiatives start with having key stakeholders on both sides engage in a joint mapping exercise of the workflow across the service supply chain, and the interdependencies in that workflow. This we have seen in several of the earlier chapters. When managers see "the whole elephant", they also realize how their own behavior indirectly increases the very performance issues with their supplier that they seek to eliminate. From such an understanding, improved service process designs can follow. KPIs that monitor performance at key points on both sides, so also on the customer side, can be very helpful here.

Common end-of-process KPIs follow logically out of the shared understanding that both sides have developed through the systemic exercise of understanding the whole service supply chain. Arriving at such an understanding takes patience and time. Again, one has to dare to go slow to go fast. Again, the guiding principle here is *festina lente*. Surely, every harbor master would agree with such a motto.

REFERENCES

Akkermans, H. A., & van Helden, K. (2002). Virtuous and vicious cycles in ERP implementation: A case study of interrelations between critical success factors. *European Journal of Information Systems, 11*(1), 35–46.

Akkermans, H., Bogerd, P., & van Doremalen, J. (2004). Travail, transparency and trust: A case study of computer-supported collaborative supply chain planning in high-tech electronics. *European Journal of Operations Research, 53*(2), 445–456.

Autry, C. W., & Golicic, S. L. (2010). Evaluating buyer–supplier relationship–performance spirals: A longitudinal study. *Journal of Operations Management, 28*, 87–100.

Choi, T. Y., & Wu, Z. (2009). Taking the leap from dyads to triads: Buyer–supplier relationships in supply networks. *Journal of Purchasing and Supply Management, 15*(4), 263–266.

Holmstrom, B., & Milgrom, P. (1991). Multi-task principal-agent analyses: Incentive contracts, asset ownership and job design. *Journal of Law, Economics and Organization, 7*(Special Issue), 24–52.

Kern, T., Willcocks, L. P., & van Heck, E. (2002). The winner's curse in IT outsourcing: Strategies for avoiding relational trauma. *California Management Review, 44*(2), 47–69.

Lacity, M. C., Khan, S. A., & Willcocks, L. P. (2009). A review of the IT outsourcing literature: Insights for practice. *The Journal of Strategic Information Systems, 18*(3), 130–146.

Parker, G. G., & Anderson, E. G. (2002). From buyer to integrator: The transformation of the supply-chain manager in the vertically disintegrating firm. *Production and Operations Management, 11*(1), 75–91.

Pieters, A. J. H. M., van Oirschot, C., & Akkermans, H. A. (2010). No cure for all evils: Dutch obstetric care and limits to the applicability of the focused factory concept in health care. *International Journal of Operations and Production Management., 30*(11), 1112–1139.

Roberts, J. (2004). *The modern firm. Organizational design for performance and growth.* Oxford: Oxford University Press.

Sampson, S. E. (2000). Customer-supplier duality and bi-directional supply chains in service organizations. *International Journal of Service Industry Management, 11*(4), 348–364.

Skinner, W. (1974). The focused factory. *Harvard Business Review, 52*(3), 113–121.

Wynstra, F., Spring, M., & Schoenherr, T. (2015). Service triads: A research agenda for buyer–supplier–customer triads in business services. *Journal of Operations Management, 35*, 1–20.

CHAPTER 8

Interactions with Government:
Regulating the Regulators

Abstract When there is no customer who is directly paying for a service, there are stakeholders who need to be managed. Often, these include the regulatory authorities. This chapter investigates the interactions between a gas and electricity utility and the regulatory authorities overseeing it and its rollout of so-called smart meters for gas and electricity. The government was requiring the utility to make haste with installing such smart meters in all homes. The utility made a great deal of haste, but was wise enough to also commission a stress test of the service supply chain. Lessons learned from this system dynamics-based stress test led to a renegotiation of the earlier targets, but also to the identification of non-obvious, high-leverage policies to speed up the rollout process.

When there is no customer who is directly paying for a service, there are stakeholders that need to be managed. Often, these include the regulatory authorities. This is the final category of stakeholders this book looks at. In this chapter we investigate the interactions between a gas and electricity utility and the regulatory authorities overseeing it. Installing a so-called smart meter for gas and electricity in a house is not a service that utilities can charge money for. However, the government may, nevertheless, require the utility to make haste with installing such smart meters in all homes.

8.1   HASTE FOR THE COMMON GOOD

Governmental Urge to Move Fast

The use of so-called smart meters for electricity and gas usage in households is seen as an important means for more conscious use of energy by consumers. And, thus, for a more durable world. Therefore, in 2014 EU legislation required union member states to ensure the implementation of smart metering under EU energy market legislation. A rollout target of 80% market penetration for electricity by 2020 was formulated.

This case zooms in on one particular utility or Distribution System Operator (DSO) for one particular European region of some two million households. The process of replacing an old meter with a more advanced, "smart" meter is called conversion. This operator formulated a very ambitious goal for its 2015 conversion rate, which amounted to over five times its conversion rate for the year 2014. It assumed that this ramp-up was feasible for its service supply chain, involving numerous front-end and back-end capacity groups with a multitude of interrelations and interdependencies between them.

Initial Underestimation of Managerial Challenge

Initially, management of the DSO assumed that it would be easy to ramp up key capacities for the rollout through outsourcing and accelerated hiring.

In a Board Briefing of November 2014 the following positive news was emphasized:

- Based on the good results with earlier in-house development of smart meter designs and firmware;
- And based on the positive results from a small-scale pilot in a rural area which were extrapolated to the metropolitan regions;
- And given the insistence of the regulator to meet the earlier agreed-upon targets,
- The overall rollout process was carved out into six separate and dedicated subprocesses with specific management focus.
- The development of a key performance indicator (KPI) dashboard and operational reports are also mentioned.
- Risks with regard to accelerated hiring of technician staff are not mentioned at this stage.

Failure to Meet Ramp-Up Targets

From the beginning of the rollout, the actual install rate remained well below target. For some time, this fact could be played down. Gradually, it became clear that the original targets were not feasible. Figure 8.1 shows time series data from the first half of 2015 that illustrates this. Consistently, the realization in the number of households to be converted stayed below the planning target. This remained so even when the planning was adjusted to reality in May of that year. Of course, in absolute numbers, this meant more and more households. However, even percentagewise, the gap kept widening, rather than closing, until after the summer.

There were multiple reasons for this, but the core two reasons were that (1) it was more difficult than expected to ramp up install technician capacity and (2) install productivity consistently stayed below the planning target. Regarding the first, these technicians had to be hired from the outside, as the own internal technicians continued to have work with the existing installed base. Regarding the second, an unrealistic install productivity number of 8 installs per day was used in the planning algorithms, despite consistent evidence that at best it was rather 6 per day. That alone implies a capacity gap of 25%.

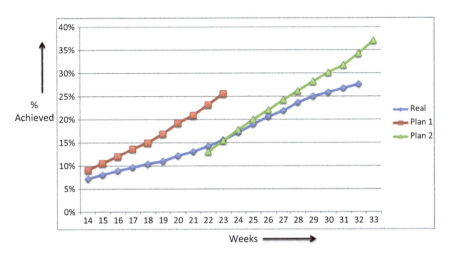

Fig. 8.1   Percentage smart meter installs planned and realized, 2015

Increased Managerial Attention

The disappointing progress led to closer attention from senior management for the rollout program. It also led to the commissioning of a so-called stress test of the rollout, in analogy with the European banking stress tests that took place around that time. The author was part of the team that developed the simulation model that was used to conduct this stress test. The analysis revealed multiple reasons why the original ramp-up schedule was not feasible, to which we will return later.

Renegotiating with the Regulator

In July, the company's CEO went back to the government agency in charge. Armed with the stress test analysis, the regulatory authorities could be convinced that sticking to the original targets was not only unrealistic, but also potentially harmful and hazardous. In the summer of 2015, the original target for 2015 was brought down by more than a third. This fallback would have to be compensated by more conversions than originally planned in 2016 and 2016. These results, backed by both data and models, gave peace of mind to the regulatory authorities and to top management alike. The original manager for the smart meter rollout, who had been responsible for the overly optimistic planning, was replaced shortly afterward. At the end of the year, the new target was reliably met. By that time, the civil servants at the regulatory authority were truly at ease.

8.2   Root Causes

- Lack of understanding of interdependencies and delays
- Lack of visibility of 2nd and 3rd order effects
- Lack of end-to-end transparency of capacity and loads
- Lack of integral service supply chain control

Lack of Understanding of Interdependencies and Delays

The complexity of the entire service supply chain was cognitively overwhelming for the various service supply chain actors. Figure 8.2 shows

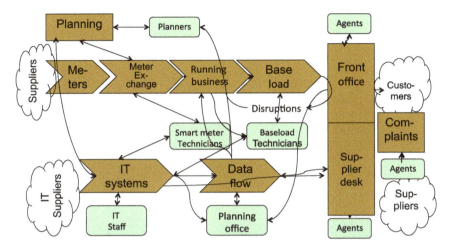

Fig. 8.2   Main service supply chain processes and their key interdependencies

its main process steps and interdependencies. It comes from a presentation to management in May 2015. Even this simplified picture shows
some twelve different stakeholders, four of them outside of the company, and ten main processes. It also shows that the primary processes of
smart meter exchange next to the base load of serving the installed base
tell only a small part of the story. There is also planning at multiple levels
(only one level shown), there is IT innovations, and there is the smart
meter data management. There is the frontoffice desk for customer queries and the supplier desk.

Last but not the least, there are all sorts of interdependencies between
these various sectors, with considerable delays.

Lack of Visibility of Indirect Effects

In this service supply chain (or should we say network or even ecosystem?)
there were direct 1st order processes but also indirect 2nd and 3rd order
processes. At first, these indirect processes weren't even taken into account.
Later on, it remained very difficult to assess the effects of the rollout on
these 2nd and 3rd order processes.

To clarify:

- 1st order: Primary order flow of smart meter exchange and base load/physical logistics supply chain/smart meter technicians and base load technicians
- 2nd order: Planning, invoicing, finance, data management
- 3rd order: customer call center, supplier desk, complaints handling, IT, innovation

In particular, the 3rd order processes were initially disregarded, whereas they might turn into serious bottlenecks later on. This was because capacity constraints in the frontoffice processes of smart meter exchange were most visible in the short run.

However, as the cumulative number of smart meters would grow, the size of the installed base compared to the new install rate would become bigger and bigger. As a result, the capacities required to handle the installed base would become more and more important, especially after the first year of the rollout.

For instance, managing the data flow and the associated IT systems would become a huge task. The capacities and capabilities required to manage these second and third order processes was much less visible. This was all the more so since the capacity issues related to the primary processes were so very visible at the time.

Lack of End-to-End Transparency of Capacity and Loads

This utility knew quite well the key capacities and loads of the highly complex electricity networks it managed. It, therefore, could easily identify bottlenecks and buffer capacities, even under changing conditions. This was not at all true for the service supply chain that was needed for the smart meter rollout. One main reason for this lack of transparency is that different units of measure apply throughout. In an electricity network, it is volts, amperes, and watt all around. But in the smart meter supply chain, it was impossible to translate smart meters into calls to the frontoffice desk, for instance. This is illustrated by Fig. 8.3.

Many of the interdependencies between departments, external partners, and consumers were not known or ignored in planning. Moreover,

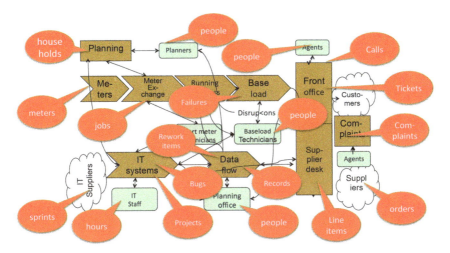

Fig. 8.3 Units of measure throughout the smart meter supply chain

for many of the key parameter values involved, there were no good estimates available. For example, if there were not enough programmers to conduct the software sprints in innovation, it would lead to more bugs. Those bugs would lead to more rework in the data flow. That would lead to delays in administrative processing, which would lead to extra queries to the call center. But how many? And when?

Lack of Integral Service Supply Chain Control

Such sophisticated but necessary planning questions were also not asked because the service supply chain lacked integral control. Back in November 2014, the smart meter rollout was split up into six independent processes, each with their own tasks and responsibilities, management, KPIs, and budgets:

- New install process
- Meter exchange process
- Energy network process
- Physical distribution process
- Reprovisioning process
- Meter data measurement process

As will have become clear by now, all these processes were closely inter-linked, and they were certainly also not complete either. Given this frag-mentation of tasks and responsibilities, it is understandable that the service supply chain really wasn't in control. What was needed was an integral and systemic approach.

8.3   SYSTEMIC SOLUTIONS

Three sets of systemic solutions were interlinked in time and logic in this case:

1. *End-to-end mapping* of the service operations (=collaborative diagnostics)
2. *Development of a stress test simulation model* with the project team and stakeholders (=collaborative redesign)
3. *Installing a Sales & Operations process* for integral service supply chain control (=collaborative process optimization).

We will discuss them in this order.

End-to-End Mapping of Service Operations

Mapping the end-to-end service supply chain created an integral and sys-temic insight of interdependencies with key staff. As early as December 2014 a group model-building session (Vennix 1996) was conducted at the DSO to map the service operations involved with the smart meter rollout. This was at an early stage, since the rollout really still had to start. This early stage was thanks to the Chief Procurement Officer (CPO) who was familiar with the approach and saw further than all other managers at this stage.

Figure 8.4 is a photograph of a typical output of such a session. It shows the complexity of a 3-hour mapping of all the relevant processes and their connections. This particular model was generated with the author as facilitator by over 20 representatives from 12 business processes within the service supply chain. Anyone who has been involved in such a system will have seen at least a glimpse of "the whole elephant". They will also understand the true complexity of the task at hand: how to ramp up such a complex network of interconnected processes.

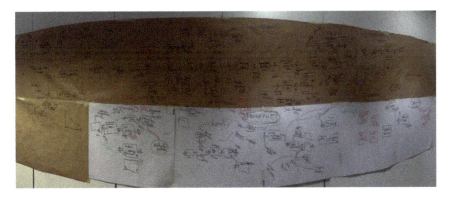

Fig. 8.4 Photograph of system dynamics diagram created in collaborative diagnostics session

However, such a mapping exercise only provides a qualitative, conceptual understanding of the interdependencies. It cannot tell which causal links are more important than the others. In the diagram, all links are equally important. For a deeper understanding, quantification is required.

Stress test of the Service Supply Chain

A simulation model of the service supply chain can reveal if projected targets are reachable. It can also identify leverage points, promising policies, for improved performance. Most importantly, it can convince the regulators that the company is doing all it can. In the first half of 2015, such a simulation model was developed by a team from the DSO, with the author as the system dynamics modeling expert.

The modeling and simulation effort yielded controversial results but was successful, nevertheless. At the formal end of the project, in July 2017, the project leader gave a presentation to management appropriately called "Less stress".

In this presentation five key stress reducers for the smart meter rollout were identified, based on the simulation analysis:

1. *Reduce administrative fallout of orders.* To the surprise of many, around half of the new meter installs met with administrative

problems after the physical install. As a result, the data processing group responsible for manually reworking order fallout was becoming fully swamped. The impact of reducing this 50% to a lower percentage was shown. It was clear that this needed to happen; else the rollout would not be sustainable. Moreover, a manifold of the data processing staff would be required.

2. *Focus IT innovation on reducing fallout.* A large part of the fallout had to do with the internal IT systems, with interfaces, with data inconsistencies, and so on. IT innovation could fix these, but this department and its IT partners were already swamped, as their services were demanded by all groups. This simulation analysis showed that full focus on this one area would achieve two things at the same time. Obviously, lower order fallout rates but also lower workloads in innovation. As we saw in Chap. 5, this would also lead to fewer bugs in other innovations, and so also to lower error rates in almost every process step, and indirectly to lower rework and so lower workloads and costs in all these other steps as well.

3. *Reduce failure rates for new meters.* It came as a shock to many that the new digital meters had much higher failure rates than the old, mechanical ones. However, the field data showed this quite convincingly. The simulation model showed the need to get this failure rate down. Else, the amount of base load would become unsustainable, with more and more often failing smart meters in the installed base.

4. *Lower workload for the smart meter capacity group.* Next to the regular technicians, a specific capacity group had been set up that would be working full time on the smart meter rollout. The simulation analyses made it clear that, with realistic productivity numbers, this group would have to deal with huge workloads to meet the targets. It showed that flattening the peak for smart meter exchange would reduce workload for this specific capacity group.

5. *Transfer ramp-up peak from 2015 to 2016.* Indeed, that would require lowering the target for 2015, and increasing the targets for 2016. As mentioned, this is also what top management suggested to the government at around this time. The simulation model confirmed that a realistic planning would flatten many of the peak workloads in primary, secondary, and tertiary processes.

Data-Driven Sale & Operations Planning Process to Manage Ramp-Up

At the end of August 2015, 3 months after the first senior management discussions of the Stress test Model findings, and 1 month after the final presentation, the smart meter rollout steering group meeting concluded the following:

1. As was predicted by the model, progress to date continues to lag behind the original plan.
2. Ramp-up speed and productivity of (internal and external) technician capacity is the primary bottleneck.
3. Rollout plans are being brought to realistic levels.
4. A basic KPI dashboard for all relevant supply chain processes is being set up (is performance red, orange or green?).
5. The findings from the stress test model guide the overview of improvement initiatives.
6. The model findings are used as direct guidelines for improvements in 2nd and 3rd order processes such as "Reduction of order fallout" and "(Internal) Expertise IT".

All this was good, but even better was that an integrated Sales & Operations Planning (S&OP) process that was set up to monitor progress of the rollout program. Here, the data from all processes, both 1st, 2nd and 3rd order processes, were monitored and integrated.

(Even-Better-Than) Expected Rollout Result

At the end of the year, the results were as foreseen by the stress test model half a year earlier. The S&OP process had carefully been monitoring service supply chain progress since then. As a result, no major quality issues or consumer dissatisfaction had occurred. The final rollout scores were even modestly higher than had been deemed feasible half a year earlier. The DSO had shown itself to be a truly reliable and thoughtful partner to the government authorities, something which was highly appreciated. Congratulations were conveyed throughout, internally as well as externally.

8.4   Conclusion

In managing relations with regulatory authorities it is worth remembering that civil servants are often seen as risk-aversive. The trick here is often not to make a mistake. Making a bold move is nice, but a failure as a result of a bold move is deadly. Predictability is key. This also applies to contacts for commercial or quasi-public organizations with the regulatory authorities.

We will never know if a public outrage would have resulted had the DSO stuck to its unrealistic ramp-up plans, with disastrous consequences toward the public in terms of leadtimes and quality of service. Fortunately, it didn't. As this case illustrates, it is possible to make a drastic change with the regulatory stakeholders, but that change should be very thoroughly motivated. And once that change is made, performance should again be quite predictable. Great performance is nice, but predictable performance is nicer, in the relation with regulatory stakeholders. They too tend to prefer a policy of *festina lente*.

Reference

Vennix, J. A. M. (1996). *Group model building: Facilitating team learning using system dynamics.* Chichester: Wiley.

CHAPTER 9

Conclusion: *No Silver Bullet*

Abstract In managing service operations with dynamic, if not disruptive behavior, there are no silver bullets. There is not one simple solution that will solve all problems. Complex services have to be addressed with a similar level of sophistication. However, the complexity in services operations need not be overwhelming. It is quite possible to ride the waves of digitized, disruptive service operations with great success. This chapter recaps that management of service operations needs to get four things right: (1) all the relevant stakeholders need to be actively involved, (2) a coherent set of policies needs to be followed, (3) with a sound appreciation of the systemic and dynamic complexities, and (4) a good balance of haste with thoughtful moderation, or *festina lente*.

In managing service operations with dynamic, if not disruptive behavior, there are no silver bullets (Mass and Berkson 1995). There is not a simple and quick solution that will solve all problems. These environments are complex places and they have to be addressed with a similar level of sophistication. In systems theory, this is called "Ashby's Law of Requisite variety": *If a system is to be stable, the number of states of its control mechanism must be greater than or equal to the number of states in the system being controlled* (Ashby 1956). So, if the environment becomes more complex, its control also becomes more complex.

© The Author(s) 2018   141
H. Akkermans, *Service Operations Dynamics*,
https://doi.org/10.1007/978-3-319-72017-3_9

However, the complexity we need to manage complexity is not over-whelming. As this book has illustrated repeatedly, it is quite possible to ride the waves of digitized, disruptive service operations with great success. The recurrent message in this book has been that management of service operations needs to get four things right:

1. In policymaking and execution, all the relevant stakeholders need to be actively involved,
2. who work from a coherent set of policies, so from both an integral and a longer-term perspective;
3. with a sound appreciation of the systemic and dynamic complexities,
4. and a good mix of "haste with thoughtful moderation", or *festina lente*.

9.1   ALL STAKEHOLDERS ALIGNED

Relevant stakeholders are easily forgotten. Especially since, usually, there are more than come immediately to mind. Every chapter in this book has zoomed in on the need for alignment with a *specific* category of stakeholders. It is time to conclude that service operations need to be aligned between *all* the relevant stakeholders.

It is easy to forget or overlook stakeholders. Here is a final anecdote. One company in the banking industry was confident it could launch a new service for terminal payments. It had already identified the key partners needed, management believed. They had thought of a terminal supplier, a telecom partner, an IT partner, and even of the terminal manufacturer.

However, a collaborative diagnostics mapping exercise with the team quickly revealed that probably the double number of external partners was within scope. When the operational processes were described that were involved with getting such a terminal up and running with customers, it became clear that local logistic service providers would also be required to get the equipment delivered. A customer care center would be needed where customers could have their queries addressed. Local repair shops would be essential to fix equipment quickly, as retail businesses cannot run when their customers cannot pay them. And the list went on, as it repeatedly has, in the cases in this book.

Top management felt that this approach was "too complicated". It couldn't possibly be all that difficult. The company went along with the original scope. And failed, because unfortunately the real world is a complicated place, like it or not.

Stakeholder management needs to be ongoing. In their seminal paper on cooperative interorganizational relationships, Ring and Van de Ven (1994) have already emphasized that in collaborative processes, everybody evaluates everybody else all the time. This is explained in more detail in Fig. 9.1. Stakeholders make assessments of the quality of the collaboration and of their counterparts through "executions", through doing work together. That always leads to some kind of "negotiations", mostly subtle, and informal, sometimes formal and not so subtle. From these negotiations result "commitments", to do more or less work together in the future. These commitments again result in new executions, and so the cycle continues. It never stops; commitments can never be taken for granted.

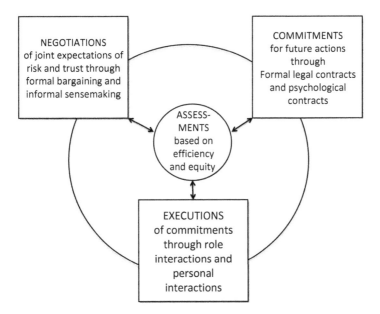

Fig. 9.1 Continuous evaluation of (inter)organizational collaboration. (Based on Ring and Van de Ven 1994)

9.2   AN INTEGRATED SET OF POLICIES

This final chapter also stresses that a single policy will not be sufficient. A coherent set of policies is needed to manage service operations dynamics well. This integration is needed at all three hierarchical levels of the organization: operational, tactical, and strategic.

At the *operational* level, execution should be seamless and integral. The customer should not see what front-line employee belongs to what partner organization; the backoffice should be seamlessly integrated with the frontoffice. The ideal is that of a stage performance, which is often created by dozens, if not over a hundred, professionals, often from a wide variety of small and large businesses, who all strive to make the customer experience an unforgettable one.

The *tactical* level of middle management is where most of the emphasis of the book has been on, simply because there is so much to gain there. This is the level where integral planning and control needs to take place. Although this practice is still in its infancy, this book advocates installing Sales & Operations Planning (S&OP) processes for service supply chains (Akkermans et al. 2016). This message comes with a number of warnings. Firstly, this certainly also includes the indirect, or secondary and tertiary, processes. The customer care center, the IT department, innovation, complaints handling, they all count. It is here that many of the major disruptions will find their origins, and it is also here that the volatility as a result of changes in the primary processes will be greatest.

Secondly, S&OP meetings should strive to move beyond the sharing of colorful Powerpoint slides. Often, it is not apparent how capacity loads in one subprocess affect loads in another subprocess in the service supply chains. Such an understanding should be made, and such calculations should be made. This is much more difficult than in manufacturing supply chains, where the MRP (Material Requirements Planning) logic is helpful. In services there is no such easy translation mechanism (Akkermans et al. 2016).

This then also explains why S&OP dashboards are often not developed from an in-depth analysis of supply chain interdependencies. It is therefore strongly advisable to have the design of such an S&OP processes be informed by a supply chain mapping and modeling exercise as described in several chapters. This will generate the early warning signals and key performance indicators (KPIs) that will benefit the chain as a whole, not just a few of the most visible parties in it.

At the *strategic* level of top management, the commitments and the deals have to be made with the leadership of all the other stakeholders. For executives at this level, it is usually really hard to appreciate the complexities of execution at the operational level. And yet, they should "go to the gemba" and try to understand why it is so hard to deliver a good service all the time. Spreadsheets and dashboards are nice, but are no excuse for not understanding the operations. They are also no excuse for not installing S&OP-like processes at the tactical level. And for the tactical level to go along fully in collaborative mode, the business agreements with top management of the other service supply chain partners need to be crystal clear as well.

9.3   A Systemic Perspective

By now it should be clear that service operations have complex dynamic coordination requirements, especially those that are partly digitized, are confronted with disruptive events, and that have to serve easily discontented customers. Such service supply chains suffer from bullwhip effects, black swan effects, and business tsunami effects.

Demand volatility in service supply chains can be many times greater than in manufacturing supply chains due to assumed infinite scalability. Moreover, *supply* volatility in service supply chains can also be many times greater than in manufacturing settings due to fallout and rework effects.

Today, very few service operations are managed from such a systemic perspective. They will have to change. An effective way to achieve this change is through a Collaborative Service Design (CSD) process, as described in multiple chapters. This can instill service operations management with a systemic perspective. In such a CSD process, the entire service supply chain is designed and managed from an integral and systemic perspective.

- It starts with a collaborative diagnostic process including group model-building with all stakeholders.
- A system dynamics simulation model developed collaboratively plays a central role in the design process.
- Secondary and tertiary service processes form an integral part of the analysis and the design process.
- Internally, specialized staff with data analysis and modeling skills is needed to sustain commitment from the design to the execution phases.

9.4   *Festina Lente* as Guiding Principle

It sounds as a paradox in these fast-changing environments, where customer preferences can be fickle, the competition often vicious, and innovation always relentless. Why should one "go slow to go fast" in such environments? Surely one has to be fast, faster than the others, to survive? As the Ancients meant it, *festina lente* does not mean "go slow". The emphasis is the other way round. Primarily, it implies being thoughtful and mindful and, while doing this, making haste, going as fast as is feasible. These may sound as two opposed ideas but, as Scott Fitzgerald once observed: *the test of a first-rate intelligence is the ability to hold two opposed ideas in mind at the same time and still retain the ability to function.*

References

Akkermans, H., Voss, C., van Oers, R., & Zhu, Q. (2016, July). *Never the twain shall meet? Simulating Sales & Operations Planning ramp-up dynamics in IT-enabled service supply chains.* Proceedings International System Dynamics Conference, TU Delft. http://www.systemdynamics.org/conferences/2016/proceed/papers/P1314.pdf

Ashby, W. R. (1956). *An introduction to cybernetics.* London: Chapman & Hall.

Mass, N., & Berkson, B. (1995). Going slow to go fast. *The McKinsey Quarterly, 4,* 19–29.

Ring, P. S., & Van de Ven, A. H. (1994). Developmental processes of cooperative interorganizational relationships. *Academy of Management Review, 19*(1), 90–118.

INDEX

© The Author(s) 2018
H. Akkermans, *Service Operations Dynamics*,
https://doi.org/10.1007/978-3-319-72017-3

GPSR Compliance
The European Union's (EU) General Product Safety Regulation (GPSR) is a set
of rules that requires consumer products to be safe and our obligations to
ensure this.

If you have any concerns about our products, you can contact us on

ProductSafety@springernature.com

In case Publisher is established outside the EU, the EU authorized
representative is:

Springer Nature Customer Service Center GmbH
Europaplatz 3
69115 Heidelberg, Germany